T
BORDE

by Michael Patrick and
Oisín Kearney

‖SAMUEL FRENCH‖

FOR AMATEUR PRODUCTION ENQUIRIES

UNITED KINGDOM AND WORLD
EXCLUDING NORTH AMERICA
licensing@concordtheatricals.co.uk

020-7054-7298

Each title is subject to availability from Concord Theatricals,
depending upon country of performance.

This work is published by Samuel French, an imprint of Concord Theatricals. Ltd

The Professional Rights in this play are controlled by Curtis Brown, Haymarket House, 28 -29 Haymarket, London, SW1Y 4SP

THE BORDER GAME was first co-produced by Prime Cut Productions and Lyric Theatre, Belfast on 2nd October 2021. The cast was as follows:

SINEAD . . . . .Liz Fitzgibbon
HENRY. . . . . Patrick McBrearty

Playwrights	Michael Patrick and Oisín Kearney
Directed by	Emma Jordan
Set Design by	Ciaran Bagnall
Lighting Design by	Zia Bergin Holly
Sound Design by	Garth McConaghie
Costume Design by	Enda Kenny
Movement Direction by	Dylan Quinn
Dramaturg	Ruth Little
Associate Designer	Tracey Lindsay
Technical Manager	Peter Milloy
Company Stage Manager	Aimee Yates
Deputy Stage Manager	Stephen Dix
Deputy Stage Manager	Sinéad Owens
Assistant Stage Manager	David Willis
Assistant Stage Manager	Emily Danby

FOR PRIME CUT PRODUCTIONS

Community Engagement Manager	Bobbi Rai-Purdy
Finance & Administration Officer	Lorraine McBrearty
Associate Producer	Natalie Murphy
Executive Producer	Una Nic Eoin

FOR LYRIC THEATRE

͏Ξxecutive Producer	Jimmy Fay
͏ͼnior Producer	Morag Keating
͏erary Manager	Rebecca Mairs
͏ͼd of Production	Adrian Mullan
͏ͼd of Development & Marketing	Claire Murray
͏ʹ of Customer Services	Julie McKegney
of Finance & HR	Micheál Meegan
͏ͽf Creative Learning	Philip Crawford

written permission of the publisher. No one shall share this title, or part of this title, to any social media or file hosting websites.

USE OF COPYRIGHTED MUSIC

A licence issued by Concord Theatricals to perform this play does not include permission to use the incidental music specified in this publication. In the United Kingdom: Where the place of performance is already licensed by the PERFORMING RIGHT SOCIETY (PRS) a return of the music used must be made to them. If the place of performance is not so licensed then application should be made to PRS for Music (www.prsformusic.com). A separate and additional licence from PHONOGRAPHIC PERFORMANCE LTD (www. ppluk.com) may be needed whenever commercial recordings are used. Outside the United Kingdom: Please contact the appropriate music licensing authority in your territory for the rights to any incidental music.

USE OF COPYRIGHTED THIRD-PARTY MATERIALS

Licensees are solely responsible for obtaining formal written permission from copyright owners to use copyrighted third-party materials (e.g., artworks, logos) in the performance of this play and are strongly cautione' to do so. If no such permission is obtained by the licensee, then ' licensee must use only original materials that the licensee owns controls. Licensees are solely responsible and liable for clearance' third-party copyrighted materials, and shall indemnify the cc owners of the play(s) and their licensing agent, Concord Theatr' against any costs, expenses, losses and liabilities arising from such copyrighted third-party materials by licensees.

IMPORTANT BILLING AND CREDIT REQUIRF

If you have obtained performance rights to this title, ' licensing agreement for important billing and credit

CAST

LIZ FITZGIBBON | SINEAD

Liz is an experienced stage and screen actor from Youghal in Co.Cork. She won the award for Best Supporting Actress at The Irish Times Theatre Awards 2019 for her performance in The Abbey & Complex co-production *Dublin Will Show You How*. Liz recently appeared in the first live show after lockdown at The Abbey Theatre *One Good Turn* directed by Emma Jordan.

TV credits include *Frank of Ireland* (Channel 4, Amazon) where she played the role of Nicola alongside Domhnall and Brian Gleeson; *Normal People* (BBC/Hulu); *The South Westerlies* (RTÉ); short film *Calving* directed by Louis Bhose (Agile Films) and feature film *Redemption of a Rogue* written and directed by Philip Doherty.

On stage, Liz has appeared as Lady Macbeth in an Irish Language *Macbeth* for Fíbín Theatre Company. Her one-woman show *Kicking All The Boxes* toured in Ireland and to The VAULT Festival in London and was also commissioned by RTE Radio Drama as a radio Play.

Performances at The Abbey Theatre include *Playboy of the Western World* by Bisi Adigun & Roddy Doyle, and *The Government Inspector* both directed by Jimmy Fay; *Bookworms* directed by Jim Culleton; *Christ Deliver Us* directed by Wayne Jordan, *Major Barbara* directed by Annabelle Comyn and *Othello* directed by Joe Dowling.

Other theatre credits include *TÓRAÍOCHT* directed by Mikel Murfi; *Remember to Breathe* directed by Orla Murphy Edinburgh Fringe Festival; Fishamble's *Inside The GPO* directed by Jim Culleton; *Twelfth Night* (Filter/RSC) directed Sean Holmes and Ferdy Roberts.

Liz Trained at the Gaiety School of Acting.

PATRICK MCBREARTY | HENRY

Born in County Donegal and currently living in Belfast, Patrick graduated from the Royal Central School of Speech and Drama in 2013.

Theatre credits include A *Midsummer Night's Dream, The Tempest* (Terra Nova); *The Real Housewives of Norn Iron* (Red Brick Road); *I Shall Wear Purple* (C21); *Colleen Bawn, Sinners, Three Sisters, Blackout, New Speak* (Lyric Theatre); *What We Are Made Of* (Tinderbox); *After The End* (Pintsize NI); *Under The Hawthorn Tree* (Cahoots NI); *Blinkered* (Sole Purpose); *Frank Pig Says Hello* (An Grianan Productions); *Importance of Being Ernest* (Wilde Festival); *Lovers* (Friel Festival).

Film/TV: *The Crown* (Netflix); *Lost City of Z* (Plan B); *Still Waters* (Carnaby Productions); *Soft Border Patrol* (BBC NI); *Spotlight* (BBC NI); *BBC Tight Shorts* (Viral).

CREATIVES

MICHAEL PATRICK | PLAYWRIGHT

Michael is a Belfast-based actor and writer. He both wrote and performed in the one man show *My Left Nut*, based on his teenage years, nominated for best show under one hour at The Dublin Fringe and won a Summerhall Lustrum Award at The Edinburgh Fringe. Other writing includes *The Alternative* (Fishamble), nominated for Irish Times Theatre Award and Writers' Guild of Ireland Award – best new play; and the TV adaptation of *My Left Nut* (BBC Three), winner RTS NI Award – best drama. Radio writing includes *This One Time On The Border* and *Quick Comedies* (Radio Ulster) and *The 100 Year Old Backstop* (BBC Radio 4).

Other acting credits include *Measure for Measure* and *The Taming of the Shrew* (Royal Shakespeare Company); *Othello* (Abbey Theatre); *Blackout* (Lyric Theatre); *Radamisto* (NI Opera); *The Complete Works of William Shakespeare Abridged* (Bruiser NI).

Michael had a leading role in the RTÉ children's comedy series *Bernard Dunne's Mythical Heroes*, and has a featured recurring role in upcoming Dutch series *The Spectacular*. He has also appeared in *Game of Thrones*, *Krypton*, *Soft Border Patrol*, *The Keeper and Bravery Under Fire*.

Michael originally studied Physics at The University of Cambridge, before training as an actor at Mountview Academy of Theatre Arts.

OISÍN KEARNEY | PLAYWRIGHT

Oisín Kearney is a writer and director who works across stage and screen and is represented by Curtis Brown. He studied Politics at The University of Cambridge.

Originally from Warrenpoint, he was co-writer of *My Left Nut* ('Show In a Bag' and BBC Three series, winner of Royal Television Society NI) and *The Alternative* (Winner of 2 Irish Time Theatre Awards and nominated for Best New Play). Oisín localised Willy Russell's *Educating Rita* and *Shirley Valentine* to Belfast for the Lyric Theatre, and worked as Assistant Director on Lyric productions from 2016-20.

Radio writing include *This One Time On The Border* and *Quick Comedies* (Radio Ulster) and *The 100 Year Old Backstop* (BBC Radio 4).

Directing credits: *Come Closer* (Summerhall Lab); *Lie Low* (ReBOOT); *New Speak* (Lyric Theatre); *I Banquo*, and *My Left Nut* (Pan Narrans & Prime Cut). Oisín has directed several documentaries for BBCNI and De Correspondent/NPO2. His first feature as Director, *BOJAYÁ: Caught In The Crossfire*, premiered at Hot Docs Film Festival in Toronto in April 2019 and was streamed by Aljazeera. He has been Assistant Producer on a number of feature documentaries, including 66 DAYS (BBC Storyville) and Oscar long-listed and Emmy-nominated ELIÁN (CNN Films).

EMMA JORDAN | DIRECTOR

Emma Jordan Prime Cut's Artistic Director has directed a strong body of critically acclaimed plays for the company, most recently Fionnuala Kennedy's *Removed* (Young At Art Belfast Children's Festival, Dublin Theatre Festival, Baboro Children's Festival and IPAY, Philadelphia. Winner Best Theatre Script-Irish Writers Guild Awards and Allianz Arts & Business Creative Communities Award); Fintan Brady's *East Belfast Boy* (The MAC, Edinburgh Fringe and Island of Ireland Tour 2018-19); *Red* by John Logan a Prime Cut-Lyric co-production (Winner of 4 Awards at the 2017 Irish Times Theatre Awards including Best Director and Best Production. Nominated for Best Director 2017 UK Theatre Awards), Stacey Gregg's *Scorch* (winner of 7 international awards including a Scotsman Fringe First, Adelaide Fringe Best Theatre Award and the 2015 Irish Times Theatre Award for Best New Play) Belfast, island of Ireland and UK Tour, the Adelaide and Edinburgh Fringe Festivals, Sweden and Germany tours. Directing credits also include *After Miss Julie* (Patrick Marber); *God Of Carnage* (Yasmina Reza); *The Conquest of Happiness* (Co-created & directed with Haris Pasovic); *I Am My Own Wife* (Doug Wright); *Blackbird* (David Harrower); *Shoot The Crow* (Owen McCafferty); *Scarborough* (Fiona Evans); *Woman and Scarecrow* (Marina Carr); *After The End* (Denis Kelly).

In 2020-21 in response the ongoing theatre lockdown Emma has directed a series of digital productions for Prime Cut including *East Belfast Boy* (Edinburgh Fringe and Eastside Arts Festival); *Father The Father* (The MAC) and *Removed* (Traverse 3 Online: Edinburgh Festival; SEODA Culture Ireland Showcase and Imaginate Festival 2021). Other digital work includes W*ake Cake* by Stacey Gregg BBC, and *Modern Myths* by Clare Dwyer Hogg for the MAC.

Emma has also directed *One Good Turn* by Una McKevitt for the Abbey Theatre, Dublin as well as *Educating Rita, Lovers* and *A Streetcar Named Desire* for the Lyric Theatre Belfast and *Lord of The Flies* for Sherman Theatre Cardiff and Theatr Clwyd.

In 2014 Emma was the recipient of the Paul Hamlyn Cultural Entrepreneurship Breakthrough Award and the Spirit of Festival Award at the Belfast International Arts Festival 2015. She won the Best Director Award for *Red* at the 2017 Irish Times Irish Theatre Award and has been nominated consecutively for Best Director at the UK Theatre Awards for *Red* and *Lovers* (2017-18) She was nominated for Best Director at the 2020 Irish Times Irish Theatre Awards for *Removed* and *A Streetcar Named Desire*.

CIARAN BAGNALL | SET DESIGNER

Ciaran is the Creative Director for Prime Cut Productions. He trained at the Royal Welsh College of Music & Drama in Cardiff and was made a Fellow of the College in 2017.

Designs for Prime Cut include, set & lighting designs for: *Father, The Father, Lady Magma, Hard to be Soft, Pulse, RED, Scorch, Secret City, The God of Carnage, Tejas Verdes, Villa, Discurso, The Conquest of Happiness, I Am My Own Wife, The Baths, Shoot the Crow, Scarborough, Woman & Scarecrow, Still Life Still.*

Lighting design for *Mydidae, Right Here Right Now, Antigone* and *After The End.*

Set Design for *Removed, Everyday I Wake Up Hopeful and East Belfast Boy.* Ciaran also filmed and acted as Director of Photography for the Digital Productions of *East Belfast Boy* and *Removed.*

Other theatre includes, set & lighting design: *The Whip* (RSC); *Peter Pan* (Hull Truck); *A Christmas Carol* (The Gate, Dublin); *The Merchant of Venice* (The Great Theatre, Shanghai); *This Beautiful Village* (Abbey Theatre Dublin, Set Design only); *The Magic Flute* (INO, Wexford Opera House, Gaiety Dublin); *A Streetcar Named Desire* (Lyric Theatre, Belfast); *The Last Yankee* (Library Theatre, Bolton); *UBU The King* (Tinderbox, MAC, Belfast); *Oliver Twist* (Hull Truck); *And Did those Feet* (Macron Stadium, Bolton); *Double Cross* (Lyric Theatre Belfast & Abbey Theatre, Dublin); *The Mai* (Irish Tour/Dublin Theatre Festival); *Lovers* (Lyric Theatre, Belfast); *The Man who fell to Pieces* (The MAC, Belfast); *The Great Gatsby* (Gate Theatre, Dublin – *Winner Best Design Irish Times Irish Theatre Awards*); *RED* (Lyric Theatre, Belfast – Winner Best Design Irish Times Irish Theatre Awards); *The Train, Observe the Sons of Ulster Marching Towards The Somme* (Abbey Theatre, Dublin); *And Did Those Feet; Ashes, Educating Rita, Two, Two 2, A View From The Bridge, Love Story, Twelfth Night, Piaf, Of Mice and Men, Tull, The Glass Menagerie, Habeas Corpus, Secret Thoughts, Oleanna* (Octagon Theatre, Bolton); *A Christmas Treasure Island, Sleeping Beauty, Cinderella* (Hull Truck); *Macbeth* (Shakespeare's Globe, London); *Singin' in the Rain* (UK Tour); *Othello* (RSC, Stratford upon Avon); *Lally the Scut,* (MAC, Belfast); *Snookered* (Bush Theatre, London); *The Killing of Sister George* (Arts Theatre, London); *A Slight Ache and Landscape* (Lyttelton Theatre, National Theatre London).

DYLAN QUINN | MOVEMENT DIRECTOR

Dylan Quinn and has been working as a Choreographer, Dance Artist, Movement Director, performer and facilitator for over 26 years. In 2009 he established Dylan Quinn Dance Theatre (DQDT) and has operated as Artistic Director for the last eleven years. Dylan has created numerous company performances and commissioned works for a range of dance and theatre companies. Dylan was Irish Times Theatre Award Nominee 2018 for his work on the production *Red* with Prime Cut and The Lyric. Dylan's work has been presented nationally and internationally across Europe and the US.

Dylan has performed and undertaken a wide range of performance, community and education projects across the UK, Ireland and Internationally. He has developed a particular focus on creating work that explores the context around the border in Ireland, it's impact and highlighting the experiences of these living in border communities. Dylan has undertaken a range on innovation projects involving performances on the border in live and film formats.

Dylan has been instrumental in initiating the We Deserve Better social engagement movement in Northern Ireland, highlighting the inadequacies of the political system. As a development of the Movement he has established the Conversations NI platform, engaging people from a range of backgrounds in conversations that are important to them and to their community.

GARTH MCCONAGHIE | SOUND DESIGNER

Garth has worked extensively as a Composer, Sound Designer, Musical Director, Arranger and Music Producer for studios, theatre, film and television. Garth's work has been performed and broadcast all over the UK, Ireland and internationally as part of theatrical productions, exhibitions, art installations, television and radio.

TV/Radio credits include: *Derry Girls* Seasons 1 and 2 (Hat Trick Productions, Channel 4); *My Mother and Other Strangers* (BBC 1); *Malaria, Comic Relief* / FIFA World Cup Closing Ceremony (BBC, Flickerpix, dir. Richard Curtis); *Days Like This* (BBC NI, nominated for IFTA); *Wee Wise Words* (BBC NI); *Not Now Farley* (BBC Learning Zone); *On the Air* (BBC NI); Ulster Volunteers (RTE); *A Year in Sex City* (DoubleBand Films/BBC 1).

Theatre Credits include: *A Night in November* (Soda Bread, Chiswick Playhouse); *Mojo Mickybo* (Bruiser); *In the Name of the Son* (Green Shoot); *A Christmas Carol* (MAC Belfast); *Rebus: Long Shadows* (Birmingham Repertory Theatre); *The Miami Showband Story* (GBL Productions, Grand Opera House, Belfast, Gaiety Theatre, Dublin); *Bouncers* (Big Telly / MAC Belfast); *Spud!* (Lyric Theatre, Belfast); *Freak Show* (Big Telly); *Tamed* (Southwark Playhouse, London); *The Elves and the Shoemaker* (MAC Belfast, Cahoots NI); *A Night In November* (Lyric Theatre, Belfast); *Penguins* (Cahoots NI, Birmingham Repertory Theatre); *Under the Hawthorn Tree* (Cahoots NI, MAC Belfast); *Hansel & Gretel* (MAC Belfast); *Aladdin* (SSE Arena, Belfast); *Nivelli's War* (Cahoots NI, New Victory Theater, Broadway, New York, Lyric theatre, Belfast); *The Faerie Thorn* (Big Telly); *Madame Geneva*

(Macha Productions); *Pinocchio* (MAC Belfast, Cahoots NI); *Macbeth* (YMT:UK, Lyric Theatre, Belfast, Edinburgh Fringe Festival, RADA Studios and Sadler's Wells Theatre); *Christmas Eve Can Kill You* (Lyric Theatre, Belfast); *Shh! We Have a Plan* (Cahoots NI, touring China, 2019); *Egg* (Cahoots NI, touring USA, 2016); *The Scarlet Web* (Big Telly); *Mistletoe & Crime* (Lyric Theatre, Belfast); *Sometimes There's Light [Sometimes There's Dark]* (Moving Dust, Asylum, London and touring, 2014); *God of Carnage* (Prime Cut Productions); *Crazy* (GBL Productions); *My English Tongue, My Irish Heart* (Green Shoot Productions); *Forget Turkey* (Lyric Theatre, Belfast).

ENDA KENNY | COSTUME DESIGNER
Enda works as a Costume Designer, Prop Costume Maker, Textile Artist and Milliner for Theatre, TV and film.

He has created work for many UK based theatres including ENO, NI Opera, ROH Covent Garden, National Theatre London and the Lyceum Theatre, London to name a few.

Previous costume design theatre credits include *One Good Turn* (Abbey 2021); *Father The Father* (Prime cut 2021); *A Streetcar Named Desire* (Lyric 2019 – Winner: Best Costume Design at the Irish Times Theatre Awards 2020); *Lovers* (Lyric 2018); *Red* (Prime Cut/Lyric 2017); *Educating Rita* (Lyric 2016) and *Scorch* (Prime Cut 2015).

Film/TV credits include *Dungeons and Dragons, The Northman and Game of Thrones*.

ZIA BERGIN-HOLLY | LIGHTING DESIGNER
Zia designs lighting and sets for theatre, dance, opera and live music. She works internationally and is based between London and Dublin. In 2017 she won the Irish Times Theatre Award for Best Lighting Design for her design of Pan Pan Theatre Company's production of *The Importance of Nothing*.

Theatre includes: As lighting designer *Skin Hunger* (Dante Or Die, Stone Nest, London); *Two* (Hull Truck); *Meat* (Theatre503); *Flights* (Project Arts Centre, Dublin/Clapham Omnibus); *Promises, Promises* (Centrál Színház, Budapest); *Ignition 19* (Frantic Assembly); *Top Hat* (Silver Blue Entertainment – Cunard Cruises); *Cleft* (Glór, Ennis/ Galway International Arts Festival/Kilkenny Arts Festival); *Bread Not Profits* (Cleeve's Factory, Limerick); *Apologia, Hand To God, The Lion In Winter* (The English Theatre, Frankfurt); *Verspertilio* (VAULT Festival/ Smock Alley, Dublin/Kings Head Theatre, London); *Ghost Girl//Gwei Mui* (Camden People's Theatre); *In These Four Walls, Totally Over You, Pravda* (Arts Ed); *The Bystander* (Junk Ensemble Irish Tour); *A Feast of Bones* (Traverse, Edinburgh/Theatre Lovett Irish Tour); *Frankie and Johnny In The Clair De Lune* (Northern Stage); *A Further Shore* (Milton Court/Lyric, Belfast); *Romeo and Juliet* (Ballet Ireland Tour);

Melt (Smock Alley, Dublin/Dublin Theatre Festival); *Annie* (Cork Opera House); *Ladykillers* (Lyric, Belfast); *The Importance of Being Earnest* (MAC, Belfast); *Benighted* (Old Red Lion); *The Importance of Nothing* – Irish Times Theatre Award for Best Lighting Design (Project Arts Centre, Dublin/Irish Tour); *The Nest* (Lyric, Belfast/Young Vic, London); *Fabric* (UK Tour); *East of Berlin* (Project Arts Centre, Dublin); *The Night Alive* (Gaiety Theatre, Dublin/Lyric, Belfast/Dublin Theatre Festival); *The Nutcracker* (Gaiety Theatre, Dublin/ Ballet Ireland UK and Irish Tour).

As Set Designer *Bullet Tongue Reloaded, Bullet Tongue* (Big House); *The Dead* (Smock Alley, Dublin). She also designed the set for the Olympia Theatre, Dublin performances of *Grace Jones* concerts for Bloodlight and Bami by Blinder Films.

As Set and Lighting Designer *Embargo* (Fishamble, Dublin); *Solar Bones* (Rough Magic, Kilkenny Arts Festival); *User Not Found* (Dante or Die UK and International Tour); *They Called Her Vivaldi* Abbey Theatre, Dublin/Theatre Lovett US and Irish Tours); *The Misfits* (The Corn Exchange, Smock Alley, Dublin/Dublin Theatre Festival); *The Shitstorm* (Abbey Theatre, Dublin/Dublin Fringe); *Before Monsters Were Made* (15th Oak Irish Tour); *Northern Star* (Project Arts Centre, Dublin/Tron, Glasgow/Lyric, Belfast); *Inhabitance* (Project Arts Centre, Dublin); *Human Child* (Smock Alley, Dublin/Underbelly/Irish Tour); *Broadening* (The Lir, Dublin/Project Arts Centre, Dublin).

Established in Belfast in 1992 Prime Cut Productions is a company limited by guarantee and a registered charity. Prime Cut is one of Northern Ireland's critically acclaimed arts organisations. Excellence is at the core of our practice and we are committed to producing artistically engaging experiences for our audiences and artists.

Prime Cut delivers under three main strands: CREATE; INNOVATE and PARTICIPATE.

- **CREATE:** The production of excellent performance and writing from Northern Ireland for an international audience

- **INNOVATE:** Driving the development of Northern Irish Performing Artists through the provision of the finest professionals training, mentorships and opportunities

- **PARTICIPATE:** The provision of a creative resource promoting autonomy and artistic self-expression for communities across Northern Ireland with trust and collaboration at its heart.

Since 2014 Prime Cut has been the recipients of 6 Core Awards including three Weston Jerwood Creative Bursaries and Artistic Director Emma Jordan awarded the Breakthrough Fund in Cultural Entrepreneurship by the Paul Hamlyn Foundation. Our touring productions and co-productions have played to audiences across Ireland, the UK, Europe, Australia and the USA to critical acclaim and 15 international awards.

Artistic Director: Emma Jordan
Executive Producer: Una Nic Eoin
Creative Director: Ciaran Bagnall
Community Engagement Manager: Bobbi Rai-Purdy
Administration & Finance Officer: Lorraine McBrearty
Associate Producer: Natalie Murphy
Associate Designer: Tracey Lindsay
Artistic Associate: Rhiann Jeffrey

Prime Cut Productions, Unit 5
8 Maxwell St, Belfast, BT12 5FB
028 9024 4004: info@primecutproductions.co.uk
www.primecutproductions.co.uk

PRINCIPAL FUNDER

LYRIC
THEATRE

The Lyric Theatre in Belfast is a playhouse for everyone to enjoy. It's a creative hub for theatre-making, a safe space for nurturing talent and has an unwavering passion for creating meaningful connections through theatre arts.

We've always done things a little differently at the Lyric. Right from its modest beginnings in 1968, this special place has been a springboard for internationally acclaimed playwrights, poets and actors. As Northern Ireland's only theatre to produce its own productions from page to stage, we care deeply about maintaining a high-quality, diverse and inclusive programme that captures the imaginations of our audiences leaving them changed, charged and empowered.

Great writing is in our bones. Building on the canon of work from previously premiered playwrights like Brian Friel, Christina Reid, Marie Jones and many more, the Lyric continues to nurture creative talent and amplify new voices.

Our New Writing Programme supports writers whose work is unique, challenging and bravely told. Featuring masterclasses with leading playwrights and a professional platform to showcase work in performance, participants will also be invited to collaborate in the creation of new commissions at the Lyric.

Michael Patrick and Oisín Kearney first worked with the Lyric on their award-winning play *The Alternative* co-developed and co-produced with Fishamble: The New Play Company as part of their nationwide A Play for Ireland initiative. We are delighted to work with them again co-producing their new work, *The Border Game*.

PATRON	LIAM NEESON OBE
EXECUTIVE PRODUCER	JIMMY FAY
SENIOR PRODUCER	MORAG KEATING
CASTING DIRECTOR	CLARE GAULT
LITERARY MANAGER	REBECCA MAIRS
PRODUCTION ASSISTANT	KERRY FITZSIMMONS
HEAD OF FINANCE & HR	MICHEÁL MEEGAN
FINANCE OFFICER	TONI HARRIS PATTON
FINANCE ASSISTANT	SINÉAD GLYMOND
FINANCE & HR ASSISTANT	BARRY LEONARD
HEAD OF DEVELOPMENT & MARKETING	CLAIRE MURRAY
MARKETING MANAGER	RACHEL LEITCH
MARKETING OFFICERS	KATIE ARMSTRONG
	LUCY BROWNLIE
DEVELOPMENT OFFICER	ÉIMEAR O'NEILL
PR & PRESS	RACHAEL HARRIOTT
HEAD OF PRODUCTION	ADRIAN MULLAN
PRODUCTION MANAGER	SIOBHÁN BARBOUR
ASSISTANT PRODUCTION MANAGER	KATE MILLER
COMPANY STAGE MANAGER	AIMEE YATES
ASSISTANT STAGE MANAGERS	LOUISE BRYANS
	STEPHEN DIX
SENIOR TECHNICIAN (LIGHTING & SOUND)	IAN VENNARD
TECHNICIANS	ADRIAN WALL
	CORENTIN WEST
SCENIC CONSTRUCTION MANAGER	COURTENAY DRAKOS
COSTUME SUPERVISOR	GILLIAN LENNOX
COSTUME ASSISTANT	ERIN CHARTERIS
HEAD OF CREATIVE LEARNING	PHILIP CRAWFORD
CREATIVE LEARNING MANAGER	PAULINE McKAY
CREATIVE LEARNING SCHOOLS CO-ORDINATOR	ERIN HOEY
HEAD OF CUSTOMER SERVICE	JULIE MCKEGNEY
CUSTOMER SERVICES MANAGER	ELLA GRIFFIN
DUTY SUPERVISOR	MARINA HAMPTON
	RONAN MCMANUS
	SIONNÁN NA NUALLAIN
BOX OFFICE SUPERVISOR	EMILY WHITE
OFFICE DEPUTY SUPERVISOR	PAUL McCAFFREY
HOUSEKEEPING	DEBBIE DUFF
	AMANDA RICHARDS
	SAMANTHA WALKER

CUSTOMER SERVICE STAFF

PAMELA ARMSTRONG
SHIREEN AZARMI
CARLA BRYSON
ELLISON CRAIG
ALANNAH CRAWFORD
ALACOQUE DAVEY
RYAN DONNELLY
SCOTT ENGLISH
MARINA HAMPTON
HOLLY HANNAWAY
DESMOND HAVLIN
CATHAL HENRY
TERESA HILL
LAUREN HUTCHINSON
MEGAN KEENAN
GERARD KELLY
CARLEY MAGEE-TOLLERTON
PATRICIA MCGREEVY
SUKE MCKEGNEY

RONAN MCMANUS
TIERNA McNALLY
CATHAN MCROBERTS
DONÁL MORGAN
SAMANTHA OBMAN
BERNADETTE OWENS
BOBBI RAI PURDY
CAELAN STOW
THOMAS WELLS
TIERNA MCNALLY
NIKI BROWNE
LIAM ROWAN
SIONNÁN NA NUALLAIN

VOLUNTEERS

JEAN DUMAS
YVONNE DUMAS
EILEEN SAUNDERS
EVELINE WILKINSON

AUTHORS' NOTE

In late January 2020, we were honoured when Prime Cut Productions selected us as the commissioned playwrights on their REVEAL programme. Prime Cut had been instrumental in encouraging us to start writing in the first place, with Emma Jordan taking us under her wing and inviting us to Tyrone Guthrie Centre in summer of 2017 to write our first play, *My Left Nut*.

We had a vague idea for a play. Something about a man and woman in a place divided by an invisible line. 2021 was fast approaching – the Irish border would simultaneously become 100 years old and the newest frontier of Europe due to Brexit. The border has been thrown into global consciousness for the first time since 1998. We are living in a time of change, with shifting social, political, and constitutional structures and we wanted to respond to that. As we looked back over 100 years of history, we asked ourselves: what do we really know about this place we come from? We set out to tell the stories of those ordinary people living along the border line, and hoped to tell a story that would be relevant to people who live along any border worldwide.

And then the COVID pandemic hit. We were stuck inside, watching the first Act of a bad disaster movie, afraid to even open our front door in case the virus creeped in. All work was cancelled. There was nothing to do but wait. And write.

During this time of uncertainty and worry, the REVEAL Programme gave us the artistic focus as well as much needed financial and emotional support. We had a purpose. We delved into the work of other writers who have set their stories along the border: the novels of Eugene McCabe, Pat McCabe, Shane Connaughton, and Benedict Kiely; the plays of George Shiels, Paul Vincent Carroll, and Vincent Woods, and even a pre-border piece as early as 1916 – DC Maher's *Partition* set in a fictional border village in an imagined future of Irish partition. We followed Colm Tóibín on his 1980s border trip in *Bad Blood*, and Garrett Carr on his expedition following Brexit in *The Rule of the Land*. We also sought international inspiration from pieces like *I am Yusuf, This Is My Brother* by Amir Nizar Zuabi, which dealt with the effects of the partition of Palestine in 1948 using haunting dream-like poetry; *Drawing the Line* by Howard Brenton, which dealt with the carving out of the India-Pakistan frontier in 1947 through the experience of a border commissioner. We also looked at stories which convey the feeling of a single place over a long time, such as Tom Stoppard's *Arcadia*, or Dylan Coburn Gray's *Citysong*.

*

The area referred to as 'borderland' encompasses a large area of land across 10 of Ireland's 32 counties, with the line itself running at just under 500km, or 310 miles. We decided to make three research trips over the summer of 2020, and when COVID restrictions eased slightly, we jumped in our two Renault Clios – Oisín's black and Michael's grey (a pure coincidence – we did not mean to coordinate our cars) and we drove around the borderlands.

For the first trip, we started in the middle, heading to probably the most ridiculous part of the border, the infamous Drummully Polyp which squiggles around like a man following a bee. Drummully is a pene-enclave of sixteen townlands of County Monaghan that is almost completely surrounded by County Fermanagh, and can only be approached through the Northern territory. It is itself a borderland between East and West, and the ancient Gaelic lordships of Arigíalla, Fear Manach and East Breifne, and is marked by slow rolling drumlin hills as if the landscape itself has buckled up against the border.

Over a couple of days, we drove around, recording interviews with locals at a social distance in Aughnacloy, Emyvale, Rosslea, Mullan village, Redhills, Belturbet, Scotshouse, and Clones. We asked these 'borderlanders' how the border had affected their attitudes, their hopes, their fears. It takes a lot for someone to trust you with their stories and we didn't want to be insensitive. Thankfully, they were extremely welcoming and gave up so much of their time to help us. We were so grateful to hear their tragic and funny tales. We heard stories of people's grannies smuggling whiskey in tea flasks, the old army checkpoint at Aughnacloy, stories from the GAA and from flute bands and the difference between the Catholic Santa and the Protestant Santa.

We visited Brackenridge's Folly, St Patrick's Chair and Well, and Castelruine at Crom – the remains of an original plantation castle that was the scene of bloody battles in the Jacobite rebellion when the water of the lake turned red with the blood of the slaughtered. On an ancient formal lawn next to the old castle, we found a pair of conjoined yew trees, a male from the 19th century and a bigger, 800 year old female, reputedly the oldest in Ireland. It seemed to us that the borderland had long been attracting natural metaphors and symbols of an entwined conflict.

Our second trip took us to the part of the border Oisín calls home – South Down, South Armagh and North Louth. A mountain land of gorse pegged down with standing stones, erratic tomb and souterrain, massrocks and hilltops, rock-ringed and cairn-topped. Once peppered with castle, fort, and sangar, now replaced with haggard hedges, stone walls, telegraph pole and metal wire, and asphalt rippling side by side on gravelly roads. The sound of tractor engines spoil the air whilst the Belfast-to-Dublin motorway hums in the distance.

We interviewed locals in Dundalk, Newry, Dromintee, Forkhill, Mullaghbawn, Jonesborough, Red Rock Orange Hall, and Keady. Many's a corrugated shed of oxblood red lies weather-bleached and rusting next to yards of scrap. Cut grass piled high in airtight plastic bales. Yellow plates. White lines. White plates. Yellow lines. Diesel flows in red and green. We heard stories of fake DVDs at Jonesborough market, boy racers in their hatchbacks, the importance of townland names and stories of teenage discos at NV nightclub.

Around this part of the border, we couldn't help but feel steeped in history and surrounded by ghosts. We observed the beginnings of the border at Narrow Water, where it creeps out of the sea, and where 18 British soldiers were blown up in 1979. We looked upon it from above at Flagstaff, where the Boundary Commissioners would have done the same when attempting to redraw the line in 1925. We drove the hill of Faughart, the birthplace of St. Brigid, and we went clay pigeon shooting on the side of Faughill Mountain, where until 2006, watchtower Romeo Two One stood on its summit.

We passed an abandoned Famine village as we climbed Bearnavave (Maeve's Gap) where Queen Maeve is said to have cut into the rock to invade Ulster and steal the brown bull in Ireland's epic *Táin Bó Cúailgne*. We drove by Clermont Carn, where Setanta famously hit a sliotar to Emain Macha, thus inventing the poc fáda. We looked up to Slieve Foy, from where Fionn mac Cumhaill slung a rock (Cloch Mór) to kill Ruscaire, the giant on the northern shore at the foot of the Mournes, and lay down to sleep, the outline of his body shaped into the rock. This place has always been borderland. Always Crossing Land. Cuchullain, Owen Roe. Edward The Bruce.

We visited the more than 5000-year-old Clontygora Court Tomb, Moyry Castle (the first border checkpoint made by the Normans) and Kilnasaggart Standing stone, which marks an early Christian graveyard on one of the five great highways (*slighe*) of ancient Ireland. We stood on the spot where the ancient kings of Ulster were crowned at Tullyhogue Fort in Tyrone, and where in 1602, Lord Mountjoy smashed the inauguration stone to symbolically end the sovereignty of the O'Neill's. A local leaving the fort told us 'There's not much to see. Just a pile of old stones'. We had gotten so wrapped up in all the history, we needed to be reminded that we were here for the people, not the old stones.

Our third trip took us to the lakelands of Fermanagh, the badlands of North Leitrim, and through the backlands of West Tyrone/East Donegal. We talked to locals in Lisnaskea, Enniskillen, Kiltyclogher, Glenfarne, Manorhamilton, Belleek, Pettigo, Bundoran, Strabane, Lifford, and Derry. We drove over the Marble Arch caves and climbed Cuilcagh's peak, queuing to get to the top. From this highland of shale and scree, we descended to wetland of shivering reeds, following the path to purgatory – the road which ultimately leads to Lough Derg. We paid a visit to the Boa Island Janus figure of a two-faced Celtic deity, written about by Seamus Heaney, and the spot where Pyper and Craig express their love for each other in Frank McGuinness' 1985 play *Observe the Sons of Ulster*.

We stopped to bounce on the springy floorboards of the Rainbow Ballroom of Romance where many locals had their first kiss. We were welcomed warmly at the Kiltyclogher Heritage Centre, where they had an exhibition about the Easter 1916 Proclamation signatory Seán MacDiarmada, and we ventured to his family cottage a few kilometers outside the village on the overgrown backroads to Corranmore. We drove past stone circles and castles, forests and over countless border bridges. And just a 15-minute drive from Derry city centre, up into the hills of Donegal, we stood at An Grianán of Aileach, an almost 4000-year-old stone fort, which was a historical centre of culture and politics during the rule of early Irish chieftains, and one of only five Irish locations marked on Ptolemy of Alexandria's 2nd century map of the world.

We spoke to a physicist who remarked that the border follows many of the rules of quantum mechanics. It is not a defined line, but a fuzzy area of probability. The more you look at it and think about it, the more it changes. Some people think of it as a hard line, others don't think it's there at all – and they can both be true. The fools, the fools, they have left us our quantum bed, and we must lie in it!

They say a hundred years was yesterday.
A century in a blink.
Six millennia to stew the brew,
The bitter stew of a boggy dew.
Time ticks by on glacial scale,
Measured in valleys and peaks.
Drawn. Trapped.
One thing becomes other.
One thing becomes neither.
A bloody meiosis,
Neurosis,
Psychosis.
We are caught.
In bottomless bog.
Soft and wet.
Reaching back through the curtain of time.
To something we can no longer see
But we can feel.

*

In total, we recorded 70 separate interviews and spoke to 100 people of various backgrounds, ages, religions, ethnicities, and sexualities, on both sides of the border. This source material was the basis for our research, the stories of real people giving voice to real experiences of the border. The title of the piece *The Border Game* was influenced by both a Cross Border Youth Drama piece 'Border Games' (part of the Leitrim Fermanagh 'Across the Lines' International Fund for Ireland cross border youth project) and a quote from a former member of security forces: "There was no border. There was only a border if you wanted to play the border game."

We were committed to respecting the stories of the people we have talked to, whilst creating an engaging and cohesive narrative that spans 100 years of history. Large epic tales of smuggling and killings seen in the news. Personal stories of love and heartbreak. Ancient mythical tales of the region. And of course, any nuanced picture of the borderland would be incomplete without Frederick the fluffy lion. He's apparently Northern Ireland's mascot, and he is real.

We worked with the incredible dramaturg Ruth Little sending her draft after draft. Thankfully, she was not perturbed by the first 'draft' we sent, which was more of a loose collection of themes than a play. Unfortunately audiences need some kind of a story. They're needy like that. Ruth encouraged us not to force a form on the piece but to let it develop organically, and we were always struck by how she could pull meaning and resonance out of what we considered to be a mess. Two readings and one workshop took us to the rehearsal draft of the play, and to all the actors and creatives who gave us their input over the last year – we cannot thank you enough. Equally a massive thanks to everyone at Prime Cut and The Lyric for believing in us to write this play and for helping us every step of the way. We couldn't have done it without them. A special thank you to Emma Jordan for her fearless approach in taking this script from page to stage. Finally, thank you to all the border people we met on our travels, the people we interviewed, and the people we bumped into along the way. Their generosity was incredible.

*

The Irish border has shaped us as human beings more than we can understand. It is, strangely, the thing that first drew us together when we met in Cambridge. It is something that has shaped our identities and just won't go away. Despite being the cause of so much conflict and political stagnation, the border region is incredibly misunderstood as a place. To Dublin, it is no man's land. To Belfast, it is a bog of culchies. To London, it is a place of bandits and criminals, if it's even thought about at all. We are obsessed about 'where we come from' and 'who we are', both on a personal and historical level, and we feel the narratives of nationality do not match the reality of lived experience. We want to make political art about what it means to be from here.

We want people to look at the border – not the politics, not the symbols, but at the real effects of an arbitrary line on the psychology of a people. From our interviews, our travels, our research – from all that work – our two characters of Sinead and Henry began to emerge from the bog. Once they arrived we needed to be true to *their* story. The Border Game is about the border. It's about its geography, its mythology, its history, its future; but all that sits in the background.

The Border Game is about Sinead and Henry – it's their story.

Over to them.

Michael Patrick & Oisín Kearney,
October 2021.

NOTES ON STAGING

The play draws upon experiences of people all along the borderline and is intentionally ambiguous as to where exactly on the border it takes place. We ask that when staging the production, you make a decision on where exactly your version is set and have the characters and accents be authentic to that part of the border.

" - " denotes an interruption by action/thought or difficulty continuing the sentence

" / " denotes an interruption by another character speaking

"..." denotes a character trailing off

This text went to press slightly before the end of rehearsals and so may differ slightly from the play as performed.

CHARACTERS

SINEAD

All characters played by Sinead:

OLD WOMAN

SINEAD'S DA

COMMENTATOR 1

TEEN SINEAD

DANCER 2

SINEAD'S MA

IRA VOLUNTEER

CONTESTANT (S)

HOST (S)

SUZIE DENT

FIELD REPORTER

YOUNG SINEAD

YOUNG DAMIAN

HENRY

All characters played by Henry:

SOUTHERN CUSTOMS MAN

GOSSIP

DRUNK FOOL

BLOW-IN

BORING BROTHER

COW

DOG

COMMENTATOR 2

TEEN HENRY

DANCER 1

NORTHERN CUSTOMS MAN

HOST (H)

CONTESTANT (H)

REPORTER

To the border.

May it last forever / Go away soon.

(Delete whichever is appropriate).

ACT ONE

*(Late morning. Early Autumn. Light slowly
rises on a grassy hill where an old manky
portacabin sits; a layer of dirt hides its off-
white colour. Nettles grow around its edges.
One of the windows has been broken. A
T-shirt is slung over the half-open door.)*

*(Next to it, a wooden stake and barbed wire
fence has been knocked down in the middle.
The posts lie in the mud. It has rained
overnight. Rubbish is scattered on the ground,
empty beer and cider cans; plastic SPAR and
MACE bags, old clothes, old bike handles, a
tyre, a broken washing machine, an animal's
skull. An old telegraph pole sits at an angle
atop the hill, now disconnected. A sign reads
'NO SHOOTING' with a few bullet holes in
it.* **SINEAD** *(mid-30s) appears from over the
horizon and walks towards us. She wears
wellies, and carries a toolbox and some empty
black rubbish bags. She listens to music
through modern Bluetooth headphones. She
knows this land well – this is her land.)*

*(She surveys the destruction, inspecting
the fence and tutting in exasperation. She
notices a fence post has been removed and sits
partially charred in the ashes of a recent fire.)*

*(***SINEAD*** puts on a pair of work gloves and
begins picking up rubbish and putting it
into one of the bin bags. She works efficiently*

1

singing along to the music on her earphones.
["THE NEWRY BIRD"] *by Jinx Lennon.*

*(**HENRY** (mid-30s) pokes his head out of the old portacabin door. He's topless, out of shape and hungover. He does not want to be seen by **SINEAD**. He creeps down the portacabin steps and looks around for his T-shirt and jacket, but he cannot find them. He notices his T-shirt hanging up on the portacabin door, but as he moves to get it, **SINEAD** turns around. **HENRY** panics and jumps behind the portacabin to hide.)*

*(**SINEAD** notices the T-shirt hanging off the door. She grabs a large screwdriver from the toolbox and charges inside to see if anyone is there. **SINEAD** comes back out, satisfied that no one is inside and takes the T-shirt off the door and throws it into a bin bag. **HENRY** accidentally steps in nettles and stings himself. In his attempts to muffle his pain, he trips and falls over. **SINEAD** hears this, and turns immediately.)*

You're trespassing!

*(**HENRY** freezes.)*

Did you tear down my fence you wee shit?! This is my land!

HENRY. I surrender.

(A moment.)

SINEAD. Henry?

HENRY. Well.

(They look at each other, lost for words.)

SINEAD. You scared the life out of me.

HENRY. You can put the weapon down now.

> (**SINEAD** *keeps the screwdriver up. She looks at* **HENRY**, *topless.* **HENRY** *points to the bin bag.* **SINEAD** *lowers the screwdriver, goes to the bin bag, opens it and takes out* **HENRY**'*s T-shirt and throws it at him.*)

It was soakin.

> (*He airs it out a bit and pulls it on.*)

Your land? Pretty sure it's your father's land, Sinead.

SINEAD. My father's land is my land.

> (*They look at each other awkwardly.*)

Did you sleep in my hut?

HENRY. Em...yeh.

SINEAD. Comfy, was it?

HENRY. Not overly.

SINEAD. Right...

HENRY. I was walking. Saw the fire. There was a lock of young ones drinking.

SINEAD. So you came up to join in?

HENRY. Naw. Have a go at them. But they scattered when they saw me. Then the rain came on. Didn't fancy traipsin' back in the wet, so...

SINEAD. Did they wreck my fence as well?

HENRY. I think so.

SINEAD. Who was it? The Carraig Loanan ones?

HENRY. (*He shakes his head.*) Dunno. Some car heads.

SINEAD. Flip sake.

HENRY. Scumbags.

SINEAD. Don't say that.

HENRY. Next thing, they'll be setting off fireworks, or knock over some young mother out walking or nick your tractor.

SINEAD. They're bored.

HENRY. They're wee shits.

I don't think it was ones from round here, to be fair.

SINEAD. I should hope not. I'd fuckin' kill them.

(*Beat. Another awkward moment.*)

It's a brave walk out this direction.

HENRY. Ach, yeh.

SINEAD. Where were you going?

HENRY. Trying to get the steps in. Shift the old Corona stone.

SINEAD. Good luck with that.

(*Beat.*)

Well, do you want anything?

HENRY. No no, I was just...

SINEAD. What?

HENRY. I'll grab my bits.

(**HENRY** *goes back into the portacabin to collect his things.* **SINEAD** *turns to her tool box.* **HENRY** *comes out again, a bit panicked.*)

You haven't seen my jacket have you?

SINEAD. What?

HENRY. My jacket.

SINEAD. No.

HENRY. Right... D'ya mind if I –?

SINEAD. Henry, I need to get this place / cleaned up.

HENRY. It's blue / with a white collar.

SINEAD. If I find it, I'll drop it into your shop.

HENRY. Right.

> (**HENRY** *takes a phone out and looks at the screen. There's no signal. He holds it up, trying to get signal.*)

Shite.

> (**HENRY** *pockets his phone. He pulls another phone from his other pocket, and does the same thing, trying to get signal.*)

Fuck sake.

SINEAD. Walk down a bit, you'll get signal.

> (**HENRY** *pockets his phone. He looks back around at the mess and then to* **SINEAD.** **SINEAD** *realises he hasn't left.*)

Did you hear me?

HENRY. Yeh.

SINEAD. So...

HENRY. Do you need a hand?

SINEAD. I'm fine.

> (**SINEAD** *attempts to lift the old washing machine, with very little success.*)

(**HENRY** *watches her, and subtly checks out her ass. She nearly catches him and he turns away.*)

HENRY. The place is a right mess hai.

SINEAD. Some prick's been fly-tipping for months.

(**SINEAD** *tries to lift again, but it does not budge. She is exhausted.*)

(**HENRY** *watches her struggle a bit more. She definitely needs help.*)

HENRY. I'll help you.

SINEAD. Go away!

HENRY. I'll just give you a hand.

SINEAD. I don't need /a hand.

HENRY. You do.

SINEAD. I don't!

HENRY. You do!

SINEAD. Henry! I'm up to *here* today. I don't have much time.

HENRY. What's the rush?

SINEAD. Bubbles's about to pop.

HENRY. Bubbles?

SINEAD. One of dad's cows. Need to get this place sorted before she starts calving.

HENRY. Well I'll help you / then.

SINEAD. No I'm grand.

HENRY. It'll be / quicker.

SINEAD. Henry, I don't need your help. Just go on home would ye?

HENRY. Ah...well... I just...

SINEAD. You just wha?

HENRY. Ach, I can't go back to the house right now.

SINEAD. Oh...?

HENRY. Yeah. So, I'll give you a hand.

(**SINEAD** *considers him.*)

Come on. You can boss me around. You love that.

SINEAD. No.

HENRY. You used to.

SINEAD. You'll only get in the way.

HENRY. No I won't.

SINEAD. Hanging out your hole.

HENRY. I'm not hungover... If anything, I'm still drunk.

(*Beat.*)

But I'm also a big strong man.

SINEAD. Are you indeed?

HENRY. Who's useful for lifting washing machines.

(**SINEAD** *looks at the washing machine and back at him.*)

SINEAD. Alright.

HENRY. You won't regret it.

SINEAD. I doubt that... But there's rules, OK?

HENRY. Naturally.

SINEAD. One: You have to do as I say. You shop people are useless at real work.

HENRY. My work has the Henry Taylor guarantee!

SINEAD. And rule number two: we're not getting into anything...personal.

HENRY. Right.

SINEAD. Whatever's going on with me, whatever's going on with you... no talking.

HENRY. No chatting at all? A bit dull.

SINEAD. I just... I don't want to...d'ya know?

HENRY. Sure. Whatever you say, Mo Mowlam.

> (**SINEAD** *doesn't rise to the challenge, and moves back to the washing machine.* **SINEAD** *puts her hands on the lip at the top of the machine.*)

SINEAD. Right, come on.

HENRY. Naw, you need to lift it from the bottom.

> (**SINEAD** *rolls her eyes and bends down to grip it at the bottom.*)

SINEAD. Right. One, two, THREE!

> (*The two of them just about manage to lift the broken washing machine.*)

HENRY. Where are we going?

SINEAD. The hut! The hut!

> (**SINEAD** *grimaces.*)

Eugh, Henry! Was that you?

HENRY. It slipped out when I lifted it!

SINEAD. Aw ye tramp! Quickly, move, move, move.

HENRY. Which side?

SINEAD. Fuck sake Henry. Smells like poo! Just move!

> *(They carry it over and tuck it into the side of the portacabin.)*

Rule number three. No farting.

HENRY. What?!

SINEAD. Smells like a dirty nappy.

HENRY. That's the Guinness for you.

SINEAD. Just put the rubbish in the bags first. Then, we'll move on to the fence.

HENRY. Sounds good.

> *(**HENRY** nods. They both pick up bin bags and start lifting rubbish.)*

She's the spit of you.

SINEAD. Who?

HENRY. The we'an.

SINEAD. Holly?

HENRY. Saw yis outside the shop yesterday.

SINEAD. Did you?

HENRY. Aye. I'd never seen her before. Absolute double of you.

SINEAD. S'pose.

HENRY. She's big.

SINEAD. Yup.

HENRY. How old's she now?

SINEAD. Two.

HENRY. Two?! Been a long time.

> *(**SINEAD** doesn't respond. They quietly sort through the detritus of rubbish. **SINEAD** picks*

> *up a few empty beer bottles, spilling out the*
> *remnants onto the ground, and tosses them*
> *to* **HENRY** *to put them in bin bags. She comes*
> *upon a ragged fluffy lion doll. She tosses it to*
> **HENRY.***)*

Awww ye can't throw this away. This is Frederick.

SINEAD. 'Frederick'?

HENRY. Have you not heard of Frederick?! Aw you need to hear about Frederick.

SINEAD. Who's 'Frederick'?

HENRY. Frederick. He's Northern Ireland's new mascot. Celebrating the centenary.

SINEAD. Fuck off.

HENRY. To show our wee country's been a 'roaring' success.

(**HENRY** *makes a playful 'roar' sound.*)

SINEAD. Jesus...

HENRY. They're doing cushions and mugs and stuff too.

SINEAD. Who's they?

HENRY. Beattie and that Belfast MP ehhh... Gavin... There's a committee.

SINEAD. I thought Lions are English?

HENRY. I think they're mainly African –

SINEAD. No, I mean like –

HENRY. – but they can be all sorts.

SINEAD. No, I mean –

HENRY. Zoos, you know.

SINEAD. They're an English symbol! What's so Irish about a lion?

HENRY. It's from your man's book. The Lion in the cupboard.

SINEAD. The Lion, the Witch and the *Wardrobe*?

HENRY. Ach, I was thinking of the Indian. He's the one in the cupboard.

>   *(Beat.)*

Maybe you could give him to Holly?

SINEAD. Nah she already has a wee teddy. A kangaroo called Maolsheachlann.

>   *(**HENRY** won't even begin to think about how that's spelled. He sets Frederick aside on the portacabin step. He ties up a bag and goes to place it by the fence.)*

No! Not there!

>   *(**SINEAD** angrily directs **HENRY** to put the bags over to the side of the portacabin.)*

HENRY. What?

SINEAD. By the hut.

HENRY. What has you clearing the place?

SINEAD. It's a mess.

HENRY. Doesn't look like you've been using it.

SINEAD. I've not been down in ages, but I've some lad from the estate agents coming to have a look the marra.

HENRY. That what you were doing up there yesterday then?

SINEAD. Aye.

HENRY. Never thought you'd sell up.

SINEAD. Not selling the whole lot – just this one.

HENRY. End of an era.

SINEAD. Yeh...a fair few stories here. Be glad to see the back of it.

HENRY. Be glad to see the profit more like.

SINEAD. Ach.

HENRY. Your family always played the border very well.

SINEAD. Did we now?

HENRY. Land both sides... That washing machine was probably put there to launder money.

(*Beat.*)

So who'd be buying it?

SINEAD. I dunno. Whoever wants it.

HENRY. Maybe I'll buy it.

SINEAD. If you can afford it.

HENRY. Build a wee house right up to the borderline.

SINEAD. On you go.

HENRY. We could have a wee cuppa over the border fence.

SINEAD. That's not the border.

HENRY. It is. You told me.

SINEAD. Only for a bit. Do you still not know where it is?

HENRY. Not here. But I'd know it on the road – slam across it enough times a day.

SINEAD. I like to keep my eye on it.

HENRY. So where is then Miss Google Maps?

SINEAD. Run across to the fence for a car-length, turns back and cuts right through the hut.

HENRY. Ah right right. And are you selling the hut too?

SINEAD. Yip.

HENRY. Ahhh, you can't get rid of the old customs hut!

SINEAD. Well, we are.

HENRY. Your dad was mad for it.

SINEAD. Still is, but sure...

HENRY. Some aul historical society might buy it.

SINEAD. A developer'll take it away and build a lock of holiday homes.

HENRY. Holiday homes?! Who the fuck wants to holiday round here?

SINEAD. Heaps of people! They'll be coming bumper to bumper up the road to get in.

HENRY. Ach, seems a shame.

>(**HENRY** *observes the old customs hut.*)

We had some nights in there, didn't we?

>(**SINEAD** *says nothing. She starts poking through the remnants of the fire – lifting half burnt logs and cardboard boxes into a bin bag. She gets ash all over herself. She is frustrated.*)

SINEAD. If I find out who did this –

HENRY. *(Interrupting.)* Ach, you can't blame yourself, Sinead.

SINEAD. I don't.

HENRY. It's up to the parents.

SINEAD. I know.

HENRY. As my dad used to say, "It's the parents who need to discipline the children, / not the teachers."

SINEAD. Not the teachers, I know.

HENRY. Holly's all that ahead of her. St. Jude's.

SINEAD. Actually... I'm thinking St Brides.

HENRY. St Bride's? Using your granny's address in the North?

SINEAD. Yeah. So?

HENRY. Nothing. Integrated is it?

SINEAD. No.

HENRY. But you were always on about Integrated schools.

SINEAD Well there aren't any around here.

HENRY. Convenient.

SINEAD. St Brides is a good school!

HENRY. Aye and it's great to see people coming over and availing of the superior British education system.

SINEAD. It's a Bunscoil actually.

HENRY. A wee bun-school. But no jam buns.

SINEAD. Henry, I'm not discussing my child's education with you! Back to work.

HENRY. Whatever you say, Angela Merkel!

(Having cleared up the bigger items of the mess, they move to one of the fence posts which had been knocked over. It's stuck fast in the ground. They lift it up and it is reluctantly released from the mud, but is still connected to the other posts by barbed wire.)

SINEAD. Get some gloves.

*(**HENRY** runs up to the toolbox. As he rushes, his foot gets sucked into the bog up to his shin. He tries pulling his leg out, but it is stuck.)*

HENRY. Agh, help!

SINEAD. Would you c'mon.

HENRY. I'm stuck!

SINEAD. Henry, stop playing.

> (**HENRY** *struggles for a few seconds to pull his
> leg out, and begins to sink further.*)

HENRY. Fuck sake! Sinead! I'M STUCK!

> (**SINEAD** *realises* **HENRY** *is actually stuck.*)

SINEAD. Fuckin shop people.

> (**SINEAD** *goes to help* **HENRY**.)

STOP STRUGGLIN! SLOWLY.

> (**SINEAD** *helps to pull* **HENRY**'s *leg out of the
> bog.*)

1, 2, 3!

> (**SINEAD** *pulls* **HENRY** *out of the bog.*)

HENRY. Get my shoe!

SINEAD. Alright, alright.

> (**SINEAD** *pulls a muddy shoe from the ground.*)

Take it.

> (**HENRY** *looks at the shoe.*)

HENRY. That's not mine.

> (*They both look at the shoe in confusion.*
> **SINEAD** *sets it down carefully, and begins
> fishing for* **HENRY**'s *shoe. After a moment, she
> finds it.*)

SINEAD. Is this it?

HENRY. Ah, it's ruined!

(**HENRY** *puts on his wet shoe.*)

HENRY. That's while boggy Sinead. Good luck building houses on that!

SINEAD. Nothin a bit of sand wouldn't fix.

HENRY. Jesus. I thought I was gonna be sucked in for a second.

SINEAD. Become a bog body? That's the border... sucking you down!

HENRY. Wise up. Shite land!

SINEAD. Maybe... but there's something there.

HENRY. Still superstitious?

SINEAD. It's not superstition when it comes to the border. You can just feel it. The air's lighter once you cross over to this side.

HENRY. What, you cross the border and there's streams of Guinness and trad music and Leprechauns sucking you off?

SINEAD. No! Leprechauns wouldn't be sucking me off.

HENRY. Well *licking you out* then.

(**HENRY** *makes a crude tongue licking gesture.*)

SINEAD. You can piss off if you're going to be carryin' on like that.

HENRY. Only having a bit of craic.

(**SINEAD** *bends down and grabs an old milk carton which had been lodged in the mud with the fencepost. She goes to move to the other side of the fence.* **HENRY** *tries to get* **SINEAD** *on his good side.*)

(Kerry accent.) Young woman, where do you think you're going?

SINEAD. What's this?

HENRY. I demand to know if you have anything to declare as you cross this customs... POST.

> (**HENRY** *indicates the fence post.*)

SINEAD. I declare that you're a big eejit getting in the way.

> (**SINEAD** *tries to walk past* **HENRY** *again.*
> **HENRY** *becomes* **SOUTHERN CUSTOMS MAN.**)

SOUTHERN CUSTOMS MAN. Young lady if you are trying to take that dairy receptacle across an international boundary, you need to pay the duty on it.

SINEAD. G'way with that!

SOUTHERN CUSTOMS MAN. I'm afraid if you refuse to pay the duty on your carton I have the right to confiscate it.

> (**HENRY** *attempts to grab the carton.*)

Shockin' the way you keep trying to get one over on me.

SINEAD. No-one wants yous.

SOUTHERN CUSTOMS MAN. Sent all the way up here from Kerry just to do a job, and you look on me like anoutcasht.

SINEAD. Doing the Black and Tans work.

SOUTHERN CUSTOMS MAN. It's the aul women that do most of the smuggling!

> (**SINEAD** *fully locks into the game – she is now* **OLD WOMAN.**)

Big bus-loads of grannies, going back and forth across the border. Egghs under their hats, flour shtuffed down their brassieres, butter shlipped into their knickers. *(To* **SINEAD**.*)* Anything to declare?!

OLD WOMAN. Who me? … No Officer.

SOUTHERN CUSTOMS MAN. Anything to declare?!

OLD WOMAN. Only my love of the Lord.

SOUTHERN CUSTOMS MAN. Anything to declare?!

OLD WOMAN. It's a free country. I go where I want.

SOUTHERN CUSTOMS MAN. Anything to declare?!

OLD WOMAN. I might have something down my knickers… but you'll have to put your hand down to check.

SOUTHERN CUSTOMS MAN. We'll have none of that chat!

OLD WOMAN. I know the rules Mr Customs man. You're not allowed to lay a hand on me.

SOUTHERN CUSTOMS MAN. No I'm not…but I am allowed to take you into my hut and ask you questions next to my nice warm fire…

> (**HENRY** *guides* **SINEAD** *over to the remnants of the fire.*)

G'wan there, feel the heat 'gainst your gams.

OLD WOMAN. Ooof! It's toasty in here. Oooohh my.

SOUTHERN CUSTOMS MAN. 'Tis a quare heat alright. What's that trickling down your leg?

> (*The butter starts to melt in* **OLD WOMAN**'s *knickers.*)

OLD WOMAN. Oh God!!! The butter's poured out of me knickers!

SOUTHERN CUSTOMS MAN. Aha! I got you! No-one gets pasht me!

OLD WOMAN. That may be so... but it's all over your good rug!

SOUTHERN CUSTOMS MAN. *(Gasps.)* Oh no! Nothing shtains like butter!

> (**HENRY** and **SINEAD** *break character and laugh at the game they've just played.*)

SINEAD. You're a still mad bastard.

HENRY. Ach, good aul craic.

SINEAD. All the auld ladies were mad for the smuggling.

HENRY. Pack of criminals.

SINEAD. You calling my granny a criminal?

HENRY. Yes.

SINEAD. Smugglin's not a crime.

HENRY. I mean it absolutely is.

SINEAD. You're only a smuggler if you get caught.

HENRY. Caught with buttery knickers!

SINEAD. Who do you think my granny was smuggling for? Straight into your granda's shop!

HENRY. The exchange rate would have been a bit different if he knew the butter was soaked in piss!

SINEAD. Your family's as steeped in it as mine.

HENRY. Steeped in piss?

SINEAD. In smuggling! Back in the 40s.

HENRY. That was patriotic smuggling. Cos of the war!

SINEAD. Ah right.

HENRY. The G.I.s'd be in pawning their chocolate...trying to court my granny!

SINEAD. *(In thick U.S. Southern drawl.)* Evening m'am, you're looking mighty fine on this here day, alright alright alright.

HENRY. "Away on! I've a fella who's swankier than any yankee. He's off fighting the Jerries and not chasing Ulster skirt!"

SINEAD. That's where you get it from.

HENRY. Every night, she would say the Lord's Prayer, and then she'd add: "Fuck Hitler Fuck Hitler and all the other bastards". She never forgave the south for being neutral. Said yous might as well have been fighting for Hitler.

SINEAD. We were too busy smuggling. Right, next post.

> *(**SINEAD** goes to lift a fence post. **HENRY** is standing on the wire the post is attached to, and so **SINEAD** cannot pull it out. **HENRY** steps off the wire and they pull a second fence post out of the mud and set it on the ground alongside the first.)*

HENRY. Is your da not about to help?

SINEAD. Ach, he's not up for this type of work any more.

HENRY. Really?

SINEAD. Doting a bit to be honest.

HENRY. Ah, shite.

SINEAD. His arthritis has gotten while bad.

HENRY. At least he's still around.

SINEAD. If I couldn't pop across for the free prescriptions, we'd be crippled.

HENRY. Literally. God bless the NHS.

SINEAD. Covid was very hard on him.

HENRY. Aw, did he get it?

SINEAD. No no, but...a few of his friends died and he couldn't go to the funerals.

> *(A moment of tension between them.* **HENRY** *prickles. Long pause.)*

HENRY. Is that right?

> **(SINEAD** *attempts to move the conversation on.)*

SINEAD. He's still afraid to leave the house. He has a pint with the cows most evenings. Grabs a few cans and says he's "away to see the girls".

HENRY. Not the worst company.

SINEAD. Pours it into a glass for them and all – thinks it's undignified to see them drinking from a can.

HENRY. What about that pregnant one? She can't be drinking?

SINEAD. Bubbles? Nah. She's a pioneer.

HENRY. Who's the father?

SINEAD. Her Spanish sugar-daddy. A big bull called Escamillo.

HENRY. I suppose you can't compete with the Spaniards.

> *(Beat.)*

Your dad was always very good to me, the whole time we were together.

SINEAD. God knows why.

HENRY. Always a gent, Paddy Kelly. When he wasn't trying to swindle me in the shop. Claiming a tenner was a twenty. Cheeky get.

SINEAD. That's his nature. Champion smuggler right there.

HENRY. Champion? Dunno about that...

SINEAD. What you saying?

HENRY. How much money did your dad actually make?

SINEAD. Loads!

HENRY. Hm.

SINEAD. What?

HENRY. Nothing. Just... I've heard all is not what it seems.

SINEAD. What'd you hear?

HENRY. "Lucky if he broke even".

SINEAD. What dirty liar have you been talking to?

HENRY. A wee birdie.

SINEAD. A wee bastard! My dad was a brilliant smuggler!

HENRY. Oh yeh?

SINEAD. He swindled the tax man out of thousands!

HENRY. He'd tell you how much he won at the Bingo, but he wouldn't tell you how much he spent at the Bingo.

SINEAD. He made heaps! Doing everythin' – Pigs, cigarettes, gates.

HENRY. Gates?

SINEAD. Field gates. Big steel yokes on his back like he was crossing the Himalayas. But the big money... was in the subsidies.

(**SINEAD** *locks in to play* **SINEAD'S DA.**)

SINEAD'S DA. Right lads. Subs are in, and I need fellas to bring my cattle from A to B. Now who's with me?!

(**HENRY** *becomes* **GOSSIP.**)

GOSSIP. Oh pick me! Pick me! Sure only last week, I got 200 cattle through the field. Then I was smuggling with Johnny Mooney, who's cheating on his wife by the way, and in fact, I was saying to my RUC friend the other day –

SINEAD'S DA. NO! Never smuggle with a gossip. NEXT!

(*HENRY becomes* **DRUNK FOOL.**)

DRUNK FOOL. (*Hiccup. Slurring his words.*) I'd definitely be up for doing a wee bit of smugglin'... just need to get another round in...

SINEAD'S DA. NO! Never smuggle with a drinker. NEXT!

(**SINEAD** *indicates to* **HENRY** *to play his next character.* **HENRY** *strolls in as* **BLOW-IN.**)

BLOW-IN. Hello... you don't know me... I'm from somewhere... far away... yes that'll do.

SINEAD'S DA. NO! Never smuggle with someone you don't know. You need someone who doesn't talk. Who doesn't drink. Who's not a stranger.

HENRY. Got it, got it.

(*HENRY becomes* **BORING BROTHER.**)

SINEAD'S DA. Some dull as dishwater eejit you've known your whole life. A real *booooring* bastard.

BORING BROTHER. Well.

SINEAD'S DA. My brother Seamus! Perfect! Now, we need to avoid the customs on the roads, so we'll bate the cattle through gaps from one field to another.

(**SINEAD** *knocks* **HENRY** *to his knees.*)

HENRY. Ah!

SINEAD'S DA. Hup boy, hup!

(**HENRY** *acquiesces to his role as* **COW**.)

COW. Mooooo.

> (**SINEAD** *ushers him back and forth. She is in control now, slapping* **HENRY** *as he goes*.)

SINEAD'S DA. Shush you! They'll hear! Get some of this down you. Spot of Guinness'll calm you. And rock salt on the lips, so you're licking instead of mooing.

> (**COW** *licks his lips with a big grin on his face.* **HENRY** *snaps into the two customs enforcers*.)

SOUTHERN CUSTOMS MAN. Give it up bai!

NORTHERN CUSTOMS MAN. We've got you surrounded!

> (**HENRY** *is* **COW** *again, but drunk*.)

COW. Mooooooooooooo.

SINEAD'S DA. It's OK girl – I know how to get out of this.

> (**SINEAD'S DA** *slaps* **COW** *on the arse.* **HENRY** *jumps out of* **COW**.)

HENRY. Argh! That was sore!

SINEAD. That's what my dad did!

HENRY. He never slapped me on the hole!

SINEAD. He sweeled the bullock's tail around his arm, gave it a whack on the arse, and was taken like Superman, back across the border.

HENRY. They didn't catch him?

SINEAD. No they did not. But the cow shit all over him. He came home, stinking to high heaven and pleased as punch. My dad was a brilliant smuggler!

HENRY. Cute Hoor.

SINEAD. What about you? Still on the double?

HENRY. Double? I'm on the triple!

SINEAD. Good man yourself.

HENRY. There was one fella I knew who did the *quadruple*.

SINEAD. He must have been exhausted.

HENRY. Aye. He's dead now.

> *(Beat.)*

SINEAD. People are always trying to earn a penny, earn a pound.

HENRY. True enough.

SINEAD. You should hear what my ma said about how it was back in the day. Used to have to split a Mars bar between her fourteen siblings.

HENRY. Fourteen?!

SINEAD. Least your ones had the shop. No shortage of Mars bars there.

HENRY. Water water everywhere, but not a drop to drink...

SINEAD. What?

HENRY. My dad used to tell a story of how he took a pack of Silvermints from the shop once and hid it in his sock drawer. Ate one a week 'til he got caught. Granda tore the head clean off him. Said "If you don't stop eating Silvermints, I'll get the dentist to pull out all your teeth." Didn't stop his love o' the mint. Just stopped him goin' to the dentist.

SINEAD. Very good. Right, wire cutters.

> *(SINEAD goes to her toolbox and takes out a pair of wire cutters. HENRY is expecting her to throw them to him, but she walks past him. He sighs to himself and walks over to the toolbox and gets another set for himself. They*

move towards the fence and begin snipping the damaged wire.)

So, why can't you go home?

HENRY. Ah, just… there's some ahhh… there's painters in.

SINEAD. Oh right…

HENRY. Aye it's a mess hai. Got a new kitchen in a while back. Only getting it painted now.

SINEAD. Sorry I just thought… thought it might be something with…?

HENRY. Jane? Ah, no. Me and Jane are all the best, all the best. She's away to her ma's just.

(**SINEAD** *doesn't fully buy it.)*

You anyone on the go?

SINEAD. Oh yeah. The toddler really brings in the men.

HENRY. There must be someone after you.

(Beat.)

What about that lad who works at your school… what's his name, Maguire?

SINEAD. Conal?

HENRY. Yeah, "The Gaelgoir". Did you and him…?

SINEAD. He's off in Australia now.

HENRY. Is that right?

SINEAD. I'd see him about the odd Christmas.

HENRY. Didn't he live round here… over there somewhere?

SINEAD. No, that was… that was Damian McKeever.

HENRY. Ah fuck.

(Silence. They resume snipping the wire.)

Here, you should put up an electric fence – that'd fairly stop the beggars!

> (**HENRY** *pretends to get an electric shock. He laughs.*)

SINEAD. Jesus Christ!

HENRY. Aha! You see?! I can still make you laugh.

SINEAD. At you, not with you.

> (*They resume working.*)

HENRY. Is Holly excited about Halloween then?

SINEAD. Ah yeh. She's a wee scaredy guts though.

HENRY. Not one for the ghost stories?

SINEAD. Not at all!

HENRY. Me neither.

SINEAD. She almost peed herself when I told her Halloween is when the spirits of the dead pass over from the otherworld.

HENRY. That's a bit heavy for a two year old.

SINEAD. I told her she needs to dress up as something really scary to ward off the spirits. But she wants to dress up as Mandy Mouse.

HENRY. Minnie Mouse?

SINEAD. No. Mandy Mouse. From Peppa Pig.

HENRY. Right. Not very scary then.

SINEAD. No, but... the issue is... Mandy Mouse... is in a wheelchair.

HENRY. OK?

SINEAD. So I said to Holly, I said, I'm not sure that's appropriate. But she was distraught. She's all like "but

Mandy Mouse goes fast! What's wrong?" And I was trippin' over my tongue saying nothing's WRONG with her, but we can't dress you up as her.

HENRY. What is wrong with that?

SINEAD. Putting my two-year-old in a wheelchair with mouse ears and send her round the country begging for sweets?

HENRY. Ach people are too sensitive these days. You can't do anything without someone getting offended.

> *(Beat.)*

SINEAD. I don't even know where I'd *get* a wheelchair.

> *(Beat.)*

HENRY. Would her dad have anything to say about that?

> *(SINEAD rolls her eyes.)*

SINEAD. Rule number two Henry.

> *(HENRY changes tack.)*

HENRY. What are you dressing up as?

SINEAD. Don't have time for that.

HENRY. Holly's a mouse / what are you?

SINEAD. *(Fed up.)* Ah for f –

HENRY. No here… I'll narrow it down, you have to be an animal.

SINEAD. Still no off button?

HENRY. Go on. What animal would you be?

> *(SINEAD ponders.)*

SINEAD. Something that'd put you in your place. A hawk or a bull or something.

HENRY. Nice. What'd I be?

SINEAD. A worm.

HENRY. A big sexy worm. Here, if *the border* was an animal, what would it be?

SINEAD. Well, a pig.

HENRY. Pig?

SINEAD. The Black Pig. An evil school teacher turned his pupils into animals, so they got their revenge and transformed him into a pig.

HENRY. Ah yeah. I hated that story. Used to scare me something shocking.

SINEAD. Scared of the Black Pig?! Coming back to get you!

(*She makes pig noises.*)

HENRY. Naw Sinead stop, creepy. I wouldn't have called the border a pig now.

SINEAD. No?

HENRY. Maybe a snake.

SINEAD. Nah, too...graceful

HENRY. Exactly. Snakes are cool.

SINEAD. Aye, but the border's not cool. It's... sneaky.

HENRY. Sneaky like a snake!

SINEAD. No... it's like a skittery wee mongrel dog or something.

(**HENRY** *pretends to be a* **DOG***, and runs up to* **SINEAD***, panting.*)

DOG. Ruff! Ruff! Ruff!

SINEAD. Get off, ya wee mutt.

*(HENRY runs around as a mongrel DOG, and
humps an invisible DOG.)*

Eurgh, you wouldn't do well at the Crufts. I'd tell ya
that.

*(SINEAD becomes COMMENTATOR 1 on a
Cruft's DOG track, HENRY struts around as
DOG.)*

COMMENTATOR 1. Coming up next is a Border Collie. Bit
of a divisive competitor, but she certainly gets people
talking. Isn't that right, Stephen?

*(DOG jumps and HENRY becomes
COMMENTATOR 2. They run around the stage
imagining the DOG jumping about, trying
to get a good view of it as it runs round the
border.)*

COMMENTATOR 2. That's right Joan! A sublime example of
an acrobatic breed, but will she remain focused today?

COMMENTATOR 1. The question on everyone's lips Stephen.
Aaaaand she's off! Enters the track at Carlingford
lough, for a straight run up to Newry... And she's veered
left at Narrow Water.

COMMENTATOR 2. *(Sucks teeth)* She's definitely gone the
wrong side of Crossmaglen there, that will cost her.
On the hilly stretch to Aughnacloy, she's jumped in the
river and now she's scaring the ducks!

COMMENTATOR 1. Back on dry land and heading south –
will she hit Clones? *(Pronounced incorrectly)*

COMMENTATOR 2. Sorry Joan, I believe it's pronounced
"Clo-*nay*".

COMMENTATOR 1. My mistake, Stephen. She's not sure
what to do there. She sniffs the air... aaaaaaand...
SHE BANKS WEST! Hugging Clo-*nay* Town, keeping

it firmly in the Free State. Nice extension all the way round! Don't you think Stephen?

COMMENTATOR 2. I do Joan! She's hitting the lakes in Fermanagh now. Leaping in and out of the water with an almost reckless abandon. Here we go – a long climb up Cuilcagh mountain, stairway to heaven as they call it, but it's been hell for some of our competitors today! Joan.

COMMENTATOR 1. Thanks Stephen! She likes bodies of water, but how does she feel about the sea? She's only five miles from Bundoran here... but NO! She veers North – straight through Belleek, like a dog in a china shop. No West Coast visits for this Border Collie.

COMMENTATOR 2. Coming into the final stretch, and she ploughs through Pettigo, just cutting that town in half... but looking desperate to relieve herself. Bit of a Paula Radcliffe situation here! Aaaand she's found a nice tree in Killeter Forest.

COMMENTATOR 1. She washes her hands and she's back on the path again! Moving towards Strabayne-Lif*ford* – and she slices them asunder as she plunges into the river. She's really haring it down the Foyle towards the city of Derry –

COMMENTATOR 2. – Londonderry! But... what's this? ... Ladies and gentlemen! She's out of the river AGAIN! Leapt out of the water and is now curling *around* the city, ploughing past Coshquin, and slips into Muff and out into the lough.

COMMENTATOR 1. And the Border Collie has finished. An unconventional track taken there... I'm seeing the time, 19:... 21... that does look to be an historical record... but I can't imagine that will last. No doubt a more sensible competitor will come along soon. Thank you.

(**HENRY** *and* **SINEAD** *come back to themselves.*)

HENRY. It's a fuckin mad aul shape.

SINEAD. Don't get too used to it. It'll be gone soon.

HENRY. Will it fuck.

SINEAD. Sure half of it's slipped out to sea.

HENRY. I'm not happy about that sea border. But, we'll get rid of that.

SINEAD. We'll see...

HENRY. You will fucking see.

SINEAD. That's what *we* said back in the day and a hundred years later it's still here. Feckin Boundary Commission. Set up to fail.

HENRY. Aye and if they'd done their bloody jobs, ironed out a few squiggles, there wouldn't have been as much trouble.

SINEAD. Still woulda been trouble. Woulda just meant the soldier who died on this fence would have died on a different one.

>   (*Beat.*)

HENRY. Was that *this* fence?

SINEAD. Well it wasn't this *exact* fence. We replaced it like... No matter where they put the border, that's where the trouble'd be.

HENRY. Well, it wouldn't have been here.

>   (*By this stage, they have removed the damaged wire from the fence, which they have placed in a pile by the washing machine.* **SINEAD** *bends down and is disgusted to find a used condom.*)

SINEAD. Ah God...

>   (**SINEAD** *uses a stick to pick up the condom.*)

HENRY. Yeoooo!

SINEAD. Eurghh. Stick it in one of the bags!

HENRY. I'm not taking that!

SINEAD. Rule number one. You have to do as I say, remember?

> (**SINEAD** *stares at* **HENRY.** *He does what he's told, taking the stick from her and delicately bringing it to the binbags at the portacabin.*)

HENRY. Maybe it's one of ours from back in the day.

SINEAD. You've no shame.

HENRY. It's not like they biodegrade.

SINEAD. Just get rid of it!

HENRY. Good to see the cross-border bucking's still going all the same.

SINEAD. Yeh, but why do they need to do it in my field?

HENRY. Where else are they gonna do it? "Hi mum. Do you mind if I do a bit of riding in the utility room?"

SINEAD. Vibrations off the tumble dryer? Parful.

> (**SINEAD** *winks.* **HENRY** *lifts a fence post.*)

I'll do it. Get me a hammer.

> (**SINEAD** *takes the fence post from* **HENRY,** *who gets the hammer.* **SINEAD** *holds the fence post in place.* **HENRY** *raises his hammer.* **SINEAD** *holds out her hand to take it.*)

HENRY. Hammerin's a man's job.

SINEAD. You don't have a clue what you're doing.

HENRY. I swing a hammer and hit the post – it's not fucking brain surgery!

SINEAD. It's my land!

HENRY. It's my country.

> (**SINEAD** *observes they are standing on the northern side of the fence. She stares at* **HENRY.** *She walks over to the other side of the fence, and puts her hand out for the hammer. He hands it over.* **SINEAD** *stubbornly hammers the fence posts in place.)*

> (**HENRY** *begins to sing* **["FOR THE BEAUTY OF THE EARTH"]*** *By John Rutter.* **SINEAD** *doesn't know what he is singing to begin with, but eventually recognizes it and is progressively amused.)*

FOR THE BEAUTY OF THE EARTH
FOR THE BEAUTY OF THE SKYES
FOR THE LOVE
WHICH FROM OUR BIRTH
OVER AND AROUND US LIES
OVER AND AROUND US LIES

> (**SINEAD** *joins in. They really play into the trills of the melody.)*

HENRY & SINEAD.
LORD OF ALL TO THEE WE RAISE
THIS OUR JOYFUL HYMN OF PRAISE.

SINEAD. John bloody Rutter, you sexy bastard! How do you remember that?

HENRY. Never leaves you.

SINEAD. Ulster Hall. Cross border choir. 2004.

---

* A license to produce [THE BORDER GAME] does not include a performance license for any third-party or copyrighted music. Licensees should create an original composition or use music in the public domain. For further information, please see Music Use Note on page 3.

HENRY. 2003! My ma clapping after all the songs when they'd specifically asked everyone not to!

SINEAD. That English conductor teaching us how to *(English RP accent.)* "pronounce".

HENRY. "If you're going to sing English songs, you need to sing in ING-LISH!"

> *(Beat.)*

I had my eye on you from the start.

SINEAD. You had your eye on anything with a pulse. Horny get.

HENRY. Not only were you the first Catholic I kissed, you were the first Southerner.

SINEAD. That's good is it?

HENRY. Pure breed.

SINEAD. Jesus Christ.

HENRY. Mum went buckdaft when she found out. God rest her. Ah but to be fair, you weren't part of that Dublin Clique.

SINEAD. Ah, the Royal Academy wankers. They were so annoyed you got a scholarship!

HENRY. I was the Prod quota. Bringing a bit of exotic energy!

SINEAD. Exotic?

HENRY. Yous love a bit of Northern prod. Georgie Best! Jamie Dornan! Big Henry Taylor!

SINEAD. Aye, the Holy Trinity of sexy huns!

HENRY. You were glad you saw me in that nightclub. Well... all the women are when they see my moves.

> *(**HENRY** does a little dance.)*

SINEAD. Where'd you learn that?

HENRY. It's in my blood. You should have seen my granda doing the Hucklebuck at the dance halls.

SINEAD. Oh yeah?

HENRY. Picking up all the weemin!

SINEAD. And riding them in the field?

HENRY. Not at all! He was a gentleman. He'd leave them as he found them.

SINEAD. Not like you then.

HENRY. Naw, I leave them satisfied.

>*(Long pause while they work. **SINEAD** grabs a bottle of water and takes a drink.)*

Here, should we whack on some old tunes?

SINEAD. Yeh – I have speakers there.

>*(**SINEAD** goes over to the tool box and pulls out a speaker, she connects her phone to it with an aux cable.)*

HENRY. Stick on something good!

SINEAD. Right. How's...about...

>*(Flicks through her phone until she picks a song – [**"MANIAC 2000"**] by Marc McCabe.)*

HENRY. TUUUUUUUUUUNE!

>*(The music hits 00:39 in the track. They are back in a nightclub rave in its heyday. They sing along to the lyrics of the song.)*

>*(**HENRY** and **SINEAD** turn to face each other – they perform a sort of "mating ritual" – stealing glances, pretending to dance with other people. It's silly and childish. They*

eventually become close enough to touch. They shout at each other over the music.)

TEEN HENRY. HEY!

TEEN SINEAD. ALRIGHT?

TEEN HENRY. YOU'RE SINEAD, AREN'T YOU!

TEEN SINEAD. YEAH! YOU'RE AT CHOIR?!

TEEN HENRY. AYE! HENRY!

TEEN SINEAD. YEAH. HEY HENRY!

(They dance some more.)

TEEN HENRY. HERE! WILL YOU SHIFT MY FRIEND?

(She looks over his shoulder and winces.)

TEEN SINEAD. NAH!

TEEN HENRY. RIGHT. WILL YOU SHIFT ME?

*(**SINEAD** falters slightly, she breaks out of the "game" temporarily, before snapping back in, pretending she doesn't hear properly.)*

TEEN SINEAD. I CAN'T HEAR YA!

TEEN HENRY. I SAID, "WILL YOU SHIFT ME?!"

*(**TEEN SINEAD** leans in to kiss **HENRY**. But the part of **SINEAD** which is outside of the game cannot bring herself to do it. She stops herself, and once again says she cannot hear.)*

TEEN SINEAD. WHAT DID YOU SAY?

*(**HENRY** realises he's gone too far in this game. They both want to get out of this game now, but part of them still wants to keep going. The music volume decreases and the track morphs*

from Maniac 2000 into a slow number from the 1950s. We are now in a 1950s Dance hall.)

DANCER 1. I said do you want to dance?

DANCER 2. That'd be nice.

(He holds out his hand and brings her into his arms. They dance slowly and tenderly.)

DANCER 1. I like your dress.

DANCER 2. Stitched it myself. So, why's a handsome man like you still here, and not off galavanting in England or America?

DANCER 1. Someone has to look after the farm. More fool me.

DANCER 2. Sure I'm not in America.

DANCER 1. You're not, no.

DANCER 2. I love the dancehall, but it's almost over.

DANCER 1. If we were at the dance in Belcoo, it'd go on till two.

DANCER 2. Well that'd be a mortal sin.

DANCER 1. Would it now?

DANCER 2. But *we're* alright – this one finishes at twelve, so it's only a venial sin.

DANCER 1. Well, we can't have you risking your eternal soul just for me.

DANCER 2. Ach, might be worth it so.

*(**HENRY** and **SINEAD** move closer together, and finally kiss. Gently at first, but slowly becomes sexual – their hands explore each other's bodies, and reach to unbutton each other's trousers. The music is quickly replaced by a child's bathtime song, maybe*

'Baby Shark'. **HENRY** *and* **SINEAD** *step away from each other, flustered.* **SINEAD** *turns off the music.)*

SINEAD. Sorry. Shuffle.

HENRY. Holly like that one?

SINEAD. Every bathtime. Never stops.

(Awkward moment.)

HENRY. It's catchy.

SINEAD. Wrecks my head.

(Awkward moment. They don't know how to acknowledge what just happened. They go to speak at the same time.)

HENRY. Shall /we get back –

SINEAD. You hungry?

HENRY. Sorry, / what'd you say?

SINEAD. To the /fence?

HENRY. Aye we /could get back to…

SINEAD. No I said /do you want a…

HENRY. What?

(Beat.)

SINEAD. Do you want a sandwich?

HENRY. Go on.

*(**SINEAD** opens out the tool box, and from the bottom, pulls up tinfoil wrapped sandwiches. She passes one to **HENRY** and they begin to munch.)*

SINEAD. Decent day.

HENRY. Yeah. Nice to be outside.

SINEAD. Aye. And no phone signal, no-ones looking me... clears the aul head.

HENRY. It does.

SINEAD. And then you came and ruined it.

HENRY. Cheers.

SINEAD. Ach I'm messing. It actually is good to see ya.

HENRY. Yeah. Thought it'd be weird, I mean it is a bit, but...

SINEAD. I'm just happy speaking to someone who isn't a toddler. Or the auld fella.

HENRY. Oh so I could have been anyone? Here's me thinking it was my natural charm.

(**SINEAD** *looks him up and down and chooses to bite her lip.*)

SINEAD. Aye.

HENRY. Is there no-one else you'd talk to? The other teachers?

SINEAD. I'd sooner talk to the cows.

HENRY. Not much chat from the school kids I suppose.

SINEAD. Ah to be fair, there's one wee lad who's good craic.

HENRY. Aye?

SINEAD. Wee Jimmy. Dya know him?

HENRY. Why would I know one of your pupils?

SINEAD. Wee Jimmy. Family moved across the border from West Belfast. We're doing historical quotes, Irish quotes, and who would have said them. So anyway, one of the quotes was "When Ireland takes her place among the nations of the world", does anybody know it? Says Wee

Jimmy: Robert Emmet. Speech from the Dock. Then,
I give them "The great are only great because we're on
our knees". Who said that? Wee Jimmy: James Larkin,
the Lockout. That's alright, that's OK. "Ireland, unfree
will never be at peace." Wee Jimmy: Padraic Pearse. So
I says to them, look at this I says, Wee Jimmy, he knows
all these quotes and none of yous know them. And he's
a northerner. And someone in the class said: "Screw
the Northerners". And I says: Who said that?! And Wee
Jimmy says: Michael Collins, signing the Treaty 1921.

(*Pause.*)

HENRY. That never happened to you.

SINEAD. It's a joke Henry! Have you lost your sense of
humour?

HENRY. Aye but I found my sense of shtyle.

SINEAD. That's what I always remember about you. The
laughs. Remember that first time I saw you after I
came back from uni?

HENRY. I'd just started working in the shop again. When
ma was sick.

SINEAD. I hadn't seen you since choir! Would have been
what, five years? And I was raging your shop didn't
have any Brunch ice creams!

HENRY. And I was like, what you after them for anyway?

SINEAD. I was dying for one! They don't have them in
England!

HENRY. And I was more of a Feast man, and I says: "Feast
/your eyes on –"

SINEAD. "Feast your eyes on this". I laughed so hard. I
didn't realise you were being serious.

HENRY. It was a good pick up line.

SINEAD. *(Laughing and mocking.)* "Feast your eyes on / this".

HENRY. It worked didn't it?

SINEAD. Ah, we had fun.

HENRY. It was more than fun Sinead.

(They sit and remember.)

SINEAD. You should come down to the youth club some time.

HENRY. What?

SINEAD. It's all women. They need a man. Male role model or whatever.

HENRY. Role model? University drop out.

SINEAD. Would you never go back?

HENRY. Ach I looked at the Open University but...

SINEAD. I'm serious. You should come down.

HENRY. Sure what would I be saying to them?

SINEAD. You could sing them a few of those choir songs?

HENRY. They wouldn't want any of that English shite.

SINEAD. Other songs then. About here.

HENRY. Jeepers, I've got it!

*(*HENRY *sings.)*

ME TYRES ARE NEARLY BALDY AND I HAVE NO TAX AT ALL
THERE'S A DROP OF RED IN THE DIESEL TANK THAT
    COULD BE MY DOWNFALL
IF THE CUSTOMS THEY ARE DIPPIN, OR THE BOYS IN BLUE
    YOU SEE
IF THEY'RE STOPPIN ROUND THE BORDER. WON'T YOU
    FLASH THE LIGHTS AT ME?

SINEAD & HENRY.
> FLASH THE LIGHTS AT ME, WON'T YOU FLASH THE
> LIGHTS AT ME?

SINEAD.
> YOU USE THE CODE OF THE BORDER ROAD

SINEAD & HENRY.
> AND FLASH THE LIGHTS AT ME!

HENRY. Would they like that one?

SINEAD. They just might.

HENRY. Maybe I'd be alright at the aul youth club then.
Crack out "Hit the diff" as well.

SINEAD. All the classics.

HENRY. Aye. Maybe.

> (*Beat.* **SINEAD** *looks at* **HENRY** *with
> compassion.*)

SINEAD. Why'd you come out here Henry?

HENRY. I said. I was walking... the painters.

> (*Beat.*)

SINEAD. Henry.

> (*Beat.*)

HENRY. I had a big fight with Jane.

SINEAD. Ah. What about?

HENRY. I ... I dunno. Just...

SINEAD. That's why you were out walking the roads at all
hours...?

HENRY. Yeah. Looking for a good spot to hang myself.

> (**SINEAD** *doesn't laugh. She is visibly upset
> and gets up to start working again.*)

Break time over?

SINEAD. I'm getting some barbed wire.

(**SINEAD** *walks inside the portacabin. After a moment, she shouts from inside.*)

SINEAD. Henry!

HENRY. Wha?

(*Silence.*)

Wha?!

(*After a moment,* **SINEAD** *appears at the door.*)

SINEAD. Found your jacket.

HENRY. Ah, brilliant. Where was it?

SINEAD. Under the wee sofa thing.

(**HENRY** *puts on his jacket and* **SINEAD** *notices him subtly pat the pocket. He relaxes. But he looks at* **SINEAD**, *unsure whether or not she knows what's in the pocket. Her mood has changed.*)

Do you need to head off now?

HENRY. No no, I'll help you finish.

SINEAD. I don't need your help HENRY.

HENRY. Ach no, sure we're almost there.

(*Beat.* **SINEAD** *stares at him, seemingly annoyed with him.* **HENRY** *stares back, trying to read her. A standoff.* **HENRY** *hangs his jacket on one of the fence posts, and continues to unspool the barbed wire.*)

SINEAD. How long have you been seeing Jane then?

HENRY. Wha?

SINEAD. Jane. Your new woman. How long yous been together?

HENRY. Uhhh... three years, just over.

SINEAD. So like a year after you dumped me then?

HENRY. About a year after we stopped seeing each other.

SINEAD. That's long enough now Henry. Sounds serious.

HENRY. Aye.

SINEAD. Hope the fight wasn't too bad...

> (**HENRY** *doesn't respond.*)

Where'd you meet her?

HENRY. Ach one of them apps.

SINEAD. I'm assuming she's your side of house?

HENRY. What does that matter?

SINEAD. I'm just curious.

HENRY. She is yeah.

SINEAD. Well that's good for you.

> (**HENRY** *ignores her and moves to the fence posts in the middle and starts putting wire around it.*)

HENRY. How's Holly's dad doing?

SINEAD. Fine.

HENRY. Conal Maguire? He is the da isn't he?

> (*Beat.*)

SINEAD. How d'ya know that?

HENRY. Everybody knows. Off in Australia, leaving you here. You and Holly any big plans to visit him?

SINEAD. Whatever happened to rule number two, Henry? Nothin personal?

HENRY. You're the one who started it.

(**SINEAD** *starts removing the wire that* **HENRY** *had placed on the fence post.*)

What are you doing?

SINEAD. Taking it down.

HENRY. What are you doing that for?

SINEAD. You fucked it up. Start at the edge.

HENRY. Aye, but don't destroy what's already there.

SINEAD. I'll destroy what I like!

HENRY. You're undoing my good work. Keep it there!

SINEAD. (*playfully*) Are you trying to install a barrier on the border?

HENRY. I'm trying to do the work!

(**HENRY** *stands in her way.* **SINEAD** *becomes* **SINEAD'S MA.**)

SINEAD'S MA. Out of my way! You can't block the border roads! It is our right to cross whenever we choose, and if you don't like it Mr. British Army man, you can piss off!

(**SINEAD** *snips the wire.*)

HENRY. British Army man?

SINEAD. You lose!

HENRY. No, hang on. That's not right.

SINEAD. Why?

HENRY. Why are you making me the British Army?

SINEAD. Why not? You were trying to stop me going across my own land.

HENRY. But we were on your side.

SINEAD. No. Your lads put up barriers, we tore them down. They blew up the roads, and we filled them in!

HENRY. They weren't *my* lads.

SINEAD. You know what I mean.

HENRY. No, Sinead I don't know what you mean.

SINEAD. Well, / I know, but you're –

HENRY. When the roads were blown, my uncle had to go twenty six miles to get / to his land on the other side.

SINEAD. The Army were on your side.

HENRY. Twenty six mile.

SINEAD. Ach but still.

HENRY. No Sinead. It was all of us, coming together, fixing the roads.

SINEAD. Right.

HENRY. Stop trying to make it something it wasn't.

SINEAD. I'm not.

HENRY. Do you even remember the roads being blown up?

SINEAD. Yeh, sort of.

HENRY. Cus I do. My uncle would bring me out to fill them in. I was only wee, but I remember. I was there. The size of the craters. It was a nightmare for people. There's a bridge outside Kilty that was blown, and men drowned trying to get across, trying to get to the pub. Three men. On separate occasions. Closing the roads was supposed to stop the killings... Don't talk about something you don't know.

(**SINEAD** *thinks.*)

SINEAD. Hedges. The hedges had grown over the closed roads... We didn't know what was down the other end. Me and Damian McKeever used to think there was a monster in there. Turns out there was just houses. We had all these neighbours we never knew existed. Eileen Moore. Wee Charlie McGann. All these new friends, just down the road.

(*An uncomfortable truce as they both try to remember.*)

HENRY. Well...

SINEAD. What's wrong with you now?

HENRY. I need to go for a slash.

SINEAD. Go behind the hut.

(**HENRY** *hops behind the portacabin. When he is relieving himself,* **SINEAD** *is tempted to fish in* **HENRY**'s *jacket pocket (which hangs from the fence). She takes out a ring box. She checks he isn't coming, and opens it, revealing an engagement ring – silver with a blue sapphire.* **SINEAD** *inspects the ring. After a moment she puts the ring on her finger and looks at it.* **HENRY** *finishes weeing and* **SINEAD** *realises the ring is stuck on her finger. She panics as* **HENRY** *comes back and tries to buy herself more time)*

SINEAD. Uhhh... here, there's wellies in the shed if you want them?

HENRY. Now you tell me! After getting my good shoes ruined!

SINEAD. Aye, sorry.

(**HENRY** *goes into the shed to get the wellies.*
SINEAD *keeps trying to remove the ring from
her finger, but she is unable to*)

HENRY. Where are they?!

SINEAD. In there somewhere.

HENRY. I can't find them.

SINEAD. Ah right. I dunno then.

HENRY. Got them!

(**HENRY** *emerges with the wellies.* **SINEAD**
hides her hand from him. **HENRY** *kicks
Frederick the lion off the portacabin step and
sits to put on the wellies.*)

HENRY. They were in the far corner

(*As* **HENRY** *puts his boots on,* **SINEAD** *tries to
take the engagement ring off her finger. But
she cannot. It's stuck. She starts to panic.*)

You coulda told me these were here before!

SINEAD. Uhuh.

HENRY. What do you think? Tucked in?

SINEAD. Tucked in, yeah..

HENRY. Sinead. Why are you selling this bitta land?

SINEAD. Cos I want rid of it.

HENRY. Big change.

SINEAD. There's some of us who want things to change,
Henry.

HENRY. What? Like a "greenway"? "Artist retreat"?

SINEAD. Why not?

HENRY. Have a bunch of tourists knocking around?

SINEAD. Why do you care so much?

HENRY. Why are so you keen to get rid of it?

SINEAD. Anything to bring some money in. There's nothing coming from Dublin or from Belfast, I tell you that.

HENRY. Fool's game.

SINEAD. This used to be the centre of things! Emhain Macha, An Grianán, Breifne – the seats of power for the Kings of Ireland. This used to be the centre, now we're the fucking edge.

HENRY. Not much you can do about "Bandit Country".

SINEAD. Ah, piss off. That annoys me too!

HENRY. What?

SINEAD. As if we're all criminals. No more Bandit Country than anywhere else. More like the Bible Belt. And anyway, that's South Armagh! Not here.

HENRY. There's plenty round here who were bandits.

SINEAD. Not *real* bandits.

HENRY. There was. You know there was.

> (*Beat.*)

What are you hiding there?

SINEAD. Nothing.

HENRY. There's something in your hand.

> (*In order to have a look at her hand,* HENRY *becomes* NORTHERN CUSTOMS MAN.)

NORTHERN CUSTOMS MAN. As a customs official, I have the right to search you.

SINEAD. Henry, I'm not hiding anything.

NORTHERN CUSTOMS MAN. Young man, I am tasked with maintaining security and have been granted search and seize powers by her majesty's government.

> (**SINEAD** *becomes* **IRA VOLUNTEER**.)

IRA VOLUNTEER. I'm a woman, you're not allowed to touch me.

NORTHERN CUSTOMS MAN. Show me your hands.

IRA VOLUNTEER. No.

NORTHERN CUSTOMS MAN. Show me your hands!

> (**SINEAD** *hides her finger and looks around.*
> *She grabs a bin bag sitting by the hut, as if*
> *it were an explosive device. She's scared and*
> *nervous.*)

IRA VOLUNTEER. I've got a bomb!

NORTHERN CUSTOMS MAN. Oh, Mrs IRA is it? We get yous all the time. I'll plant it for you!

> (**HENRY** *grabs the bin bag from* **SINEAD** *and*
> *throws it into the customs hut. As he throws*
> *it in a fuse starts hissing. He immediately*
> *turns and sees the ring on her finger.*)

HENRY. What's that?

SINEAD. What?

HENRY. Your hand.

SINEAD. What about it?

HENRY. Show me your hand.

SINEAD. Henry, I –

> (**HENRY** *goes to his jacket and takes out the*
> *ring box, opens it, to find it empty. He turns*

to **SINEAD**, *who reveals her hand with the ring on it to* **HENRY**.)

HENRY. What the fuck are you doing Sinead?

SINEAD. It got stuck.

HENRY. Take it off!

SINEAD. I can't.

HENRY. Take it off. Now!

(Sound effects of an explosion. The portacabin explodes open. A flash of white light. Blackout. Voices begin to emanate from the stage, men, women, old and young, all sharing experiences of violence on the border. No story is heard distinctly, it all blends together. Amidst the snippets of voices, the sound of a gun-battle fades in. A streak of red light in the sky. Another. Many streaks of red light, some appearing to come out in the audience. They are tracers on bullets. It is strangely beautiful. Fade up on **SINEAD** *and* **HENRY**. *We are in a different register; things are slower, softer, more still.)*

SINEAD. I remember one night as a child watching the bullets fly. The tracers. No matter where you are, if a tracer's in the air, you think it's coming directly at you. The boys would be taking pot shots at the Brits, and they'd be firing back. My ma would run out and grab us and throw us down behind the bath... The bullets out there cutting through flesh and bone, they weren't gonna come through the bath! Then around Christmas, the Brits dug up our front garden and put a bunker in the driveway. I was just annoyed I couldn't play outside any more.

HENRY. We were the only Protestant shop in the village. Not that it mattered. Everyone did their shopping wherever. The difference, was with the Army. Young

English fellas would be looking to buy cigarettes, and the Catholic shops refused to serve them, so they all came to us. My dad served anyone. Some people didn't like that.

SINEAD. My dad had taken me to the Santi parade in town, but he told me: That's not your Santi. That's the Protestant Santi. You just knew cus our Santi, when he came he wasn't as well dickied up. He hadn't the same backing. Dad had the turkey from the butchers under his arm when we got home, and one of the soldiers wanted to search him. But dad, he threw the head up and he said something to the soldier and the soldier smacked him with his gun. My dad was choking for air. In his own front garden. The Christmas turkey in the gravel. I actually thought our Santi wasn't gonna come because the British Army was in our driveway. So my mother went out screaming to them to leave us alone... never mind the Ra, you should've seen my ma on a bad day. That's what finally got them out, and I could play in the garden again.

HENRY. First time it happened, they came along with a creamery can. They told my dad to leave. He did. Police were called. The bomb disposal expert went in and brought it into the street. Controlled explosion. I found it exciting...waiting for the bang. It happened a couple more times, every few months like clockwork. They'd call down with a bomb and the Army would come out and take it away. It wasn't exciting any more. I just took it to be normal.

SINEAD. We were playing Stuck in the Mud. Me and Damian McKeever. He was always so fast, but I was on and I caught him. And then Damian spotted him. A soldier. A man. Tangled up in our fence. Missing half his head. We thought the Provos had got him. But he'd shot himself. His rifle went off by accident. It wasn't suicide.

HENRY. They told him all he needed to do was stop selling to the Army. But my dad was a stubborn man, and he refused to let the IRA tell him how to run his business. We started getting phone calls. I remember one time his face went white...he could hear the clicks of the Army listening in, but still the voice had no qualms about saying: "We know where you are. We'll get you yet." And I thought, if they want Ireland, they can have it, but leave my dad alone. And then one day, they came in with their bomb, and my dad refused to leave. So they shot him. My uncle told me when I was watching Family Fortunes.

(*Beat.*)

Why'd they have to do that?

SINEAD. It was on the news.

HENRY. Why'd they go after a shopkeeper for selling cigarettes?

SINEAD. It was on the news for fifteen seconds.

HENRY. Did they really think if the Army couldn't get their nicotine, they'd pack up and go home?

SINEAD. Our field was on the news for fifteen seconds.

HENRY. They didn't even plant their bomb. They just left him there. Slumped over the counter. Bleeding over the sweets. Blood dripping down onto the Silvermints.

SINEAD. The soldier's parents came over. They were lovely people. Very quiet. At least the view's beautiful. That's what they said when my da brought them out here. Kept going on and on about the view.

> (*A gust of wind and the sound of a helicopter.* **SINEAD** *ducks low as it passes, pretending to aim at it with an imaginary rocket launcher. She fires, misses, reloads.*)

HENRY. The fella who shot him escaped across to the south. Sat up at some bar and sank his pint and thought he was a patriot and a hero... Then they caught him. Then they let him out. I saw him on the street a couple of times. Skinny McGuigan they called him. A young enough fella. My father would have been religious and all. Forgiveness and forget. But I could never forgive him for what he did. Then took the coward's way out. Couldn't bear it any longer. The love of one's country is a terrible thing.

(SINEAD *finally hits the helicopter with her rocket launcher. The sound of blades whirring as the helicopter crashes to the ground.*)

(*The lights fade back to normal and* SINEAD *and* HENRY *are back in reality, but the cabin is still exploded. They do not acknowledge this.*)

HENRY. Take it off!

SINEAD. I can't.

HENRY. Take it off. Now!

SINEAD. It's stuck.

HENRY. Unstick it then!

SINEAD. I'm trying.

HENRY. What were you doing, putting it on?

SINEAD. What were you doing kissing me?

HENRY. You kissed me!

SINEAD. I'm not in a relationship, am I?

HENRY. Take it off!

SINEAD. Marriage? I didn't expect you to be doing that.

HENRY. I haven't done it yet.

SINEAD. Why are you even up here Henry?

HENRY. I was walking –

SINEAD. Like what is this? One last hurrah before you settle down with the wife?

HENRY. You made me come up here.

SINEAD. Sorry... I made you? *You* showed up in *my* field.

HENRY. After you ignored me.

SINEAD. When?

HENRY. Yesterday. Outside the shop.

SINEAD. Your shop?

HENRY. Yes!

SINEAD. Henry, I don't have a fuckin clue what you're talking about!

(Pause.)

HENRY. I was in the shop yesterday, and I saw you and Holly. I hadn't seen you in...years. And there you are with a child.

SINEAD. I was at the estate agents.

HENRY. You picked her up and ran away. It was like you just had to come and rub my nose in it.

SINEAD. Rub your nose in what?

HENRY. Sinead... I'd never seen her before.

SINEAD. So?

HENRY. I knew you had a wee girl. But I hadn't seen her. When I heard you were pregnant I thought...

SINEAD. She's not yours.

HENRY. I know, I know.

SINEAD. She's definitely not yours.

HENRY. I know! But part of me went "what if".

SINEAD. None of this explains why you're up here with an engagement ring!

HENRY. Seeing Holly. It fucked me up. I threw the head up at Jane. You know me, naught to ninety. Looking for an argument. Went to the pub, sat there on me own till closing. Came out here.

    (Beat.)

SINEAD. You came up here because you saw Holly outside your shop?

HENRY. Stop saying "your shop".

SINEAD. It is your shop.

HENRY. It's not "my shop". It's a fuckin MACE now!

SINEAD. Alright.

HENRY. It used to have my name on it. It used to be Taylor's, now it's a chain.

SINEAD. But why did /you come up here Henry?

HENRY. My uncle had to sell it to give my mother something to *survive*.

SINEAD. Were you trying to / get back with me?

HENRY. The street my dad was murdered on, now has a sign in Irish!

SINEAD. Coming up to kiss me /even though you're with Jane?

HENRY. And you're selling the customs hut. There'll be nothing left!

SINEAD. And what does the hut have to do with anything?!

HENRY. There's nothing here that's mine anymore!

    (Beat.)

Seeing you and Holly...that's what we...that's what I wanted. With you. We could have had that. If you didn't ruin it...

SINEAD. I ruined it?

HENRY. Yeah. By what you did.

SINEAD. You broke up with me.

HENRY. You gave me no choice. You ruined it. And you know you ruined it. Why else would you avoid me all the time?

SINEAD. I've got my own life.

HENRY. You were avoiding me!

SINEAD. I didn't want it to be awkward.

HENRY. Ah, well top marks for that.

SINEAD. Obviously I was right, the way you're getting on.

HENRY. You haven't been in that shop in three years.

SINEAD. COVID.

HENRY. Aye COVID's a good excuse for being selfish, isn't it? Anytime you're in town, you're always speeding off. Cus you're scared of bumping into me.

SINEAD. You broke my heart. What did you expect me to do? Dander into the shop and pretend everything was OK?! Of course I was avoiding you.

HENRY. You ran away from the shop, just like you ran away from us.

SINEAD. You dumped me and cut me out.

HENRY. You were wrong!

SINEAD. Who ends a seven year relationship just like that?

HENRY. You!

SINEAD. You wouldn't even listen to me.

HENRY. There's nothing you coulda said.

SINEAD. Nothing?!

HENRY. Nothing. You were wrong.

SINEAD. Never change your tune. That's the Unionist way.

HENRY. Are you joking?

SINEAD. "We will not budge one inch!"

HENRY. You're turning this /into a –

SINEAD. The "settler" will not be moved.

HENRY. Settler? My family have been in /Ireland for 400 years!

SINEAD. Never! Never! Never!

HENRY. They fled north from Monaghan in 1921!

SINEAD. Oh, like the Serbs of Kosovo, was it?

HENRY. This is it. You wanted me to break up with you.

SINEAD. Did I?

HENRY. You didn't want my child. Cus you didn't want a Protestant child.

SINEAD. Ah yeah, cus then they'd be a fuckin prick like you.

HENRY. Well maybe it's good I didn't have a *Catholic* child.

SINEAD. Oh yeah, why's that?

HENRY. Cus they'd only want me to molest them!

(*Beat.*)

SINEAD. Fuck me.

HENRY. Fuckin' Catholics.

SINEAD. Are you blaming children for getting molested? That's low, even for you.

HENRY. You saying those we'ans weren't diddled?

SINEAD. I'm saying it wasn't their fault. Jesus, /Henry.

HENRY. But the church did it!

SINEAD. I know.

HENRY. Your church!

SINEAD. I hate the Catholic Church!

HENRY. Well if you hate church so much, you shouldn't've gone to that funeral.

> *(Beat.)*

You shouldn't've gone to that funeral.

SINEAD. I had to.

HENRY. No you didn't. You didn't have to go to the funeral of the man who murdered my dad.

> *(Beat.)*

SINEAD. Yes I did.

> *(**HENRY** takes a breath.)*

HENRY. Fuck you and your Fenian runt.

> *(They stare at each other for a long time in silence. **SINEAD** finally manages to pull the ring from her finger. **SINEAD** tosses the ring into the muck.)*

SINEAD. Get off my land.

> *(Rumbling. A border line of light spills out from the fence as the stage appears to tear apart. The sound builds to a climax before cutting out to complete silence.)*

> *(Blackout.)*

ACT TWO

(Lights up. We are in a different register. The same field, but feels like a different space.)

*(**SINEAD** and **HENRY** stand in front of each other, wearing bull horns on their heads that are locked together. The horns should be created out of objects from the space; barbed wire, bicycle handles, wood, bone, tools etc. They wrestle for a time before separating.)*

*(The two bulls own their spaces. They walk with their chests out. In control. They snort. They sniff the air. They begin circling. This dangerous competition lasts some time. They relax, they charge, clash, gash, and run back and forth. We see the external battle between bulls – and what they give and take – but also the internal battle of **HENRY** and **SINEAD**.)*

*(**SINEAD** takes off her horns, and becomes human. She looks at **HENRY**, she speaks to him, sometimes able to control him, sometimes not. We should feel sorry for the loss of their relationship – the fears, the regrets, the selfishness and the hurt. She speaks to him and commands him using only the words "Back" and "Stop".)*

SINEAD. Back. Stop. Back. Stop. Back back back. Stop. Stop stop stop stop. Back. Back.

*(**HENRY** charges at her.)*

Stop.

> (**HENRY** *stops right in front of her face.*)

Stop.

> (**SINEAD** *removes* **HENRY**'*s horns. Two humans face each other.* **HENRY** *starts tearing up clumps of muck looking for the ring.*)

HENRY. Fuck sake Sinead!

SINEAD. It's your own fault.

HENRY. Can't believe you did that.

SINEAD. You're a pig.

HENRY. Help me look for this ring.

SINEAD. I'm not helping you.

HENRY. Why did you do that?

SINEAD. Cus you're a scumbag.

> (**HENRY** *continues to search in the muck.*)

HENRY. Just help me would you?

SINEAD. Sorry Henry. I have to go look after my "Fenian Runt".

HENRY. You shouldn't have thrown it in the muck.

SINEAD. It's not like it's dear.

HENRY. What?

SINEAD. You couldn't even fork out for a diamond one?

HENRY. It's silver and sapphire.

SINEAD. Get another one.

HENRY. I can't. It's... I got it specially made.

SINEAD. Do it again.

HENRY. I had to go to Dublin.

SINEAD. Ooooh Dublin! You should have said.

HENRY. It's far enough now Sinead.

SINEAD. Three months on a steam-ship was it?

HENRY. It took the whole day!

SINEAD. What, on the back of a camel?

HENRY. How am I supposed to propose to Jane now?

SINEAD. Like you were gonna do it anyway.

HENRY. I was. I am.

SINEAD. You've a funny way of going about it.

HENRY. What?

SINEAD. Kissing me.

HENRY. You kissed me!

SINEAD. What do you want from me Henry?

> (*Beat.* **HENRY** *searches.*)

Well?

> (*Beat.*)

If you want to propose to Jane, why'd you come here?

HENRY. I dunno.

SINEAD. Do you need my permission?

HENRY. No.

SINEAD. Cos go ahead. It's got nothing to do with me.

HENRY. No look, I can't, I can't yet.

SINEAD. Why not?

HENRY. What if she says no?

SINEAD. Why would she say no?

HENRY. She might.

SINEAD. Why'd you buy the ring then?

HENRY. What?

SINEAD. Why would you buy a ring...

HENRY. I dunno.

SINEAD. ...without knowing she'd say yes?

HENRY. How do I know what women are thinking?

SINEAD. Well you're going out with the girl!

HENRY. I know I am but... so?

SINEAD. Why would she say no?

HENRY. Because you did.

SINEAD. I did?

> (*Beat.*)

What do you mean "I did"?

HENRY. You said "no" to me. When you went to the funeral of the bastard who murdered my dad. That was you saying "no".

SINEAD. It wasn't.

HENRY. It was. That was you saying you didn't want to be my wife!

SINEAD. You never asked me to marry you!

HENRY. I was going to.

> (*Beat.* **HENRY** *stops searching.*)

I bought that ring for you.

> (*Beat.*)

SINEAD. Wise up.

HENRY. It's true.

SINEAD. *That* ring?

HENRY. Yeah.

SINEAD. I thought it was for Jane?

HENRY. It is. But...

SINEAD. Sorry Henry, I just need a... hold on a second. You bought that ring when we were going out?

HENRY. Yeah.

SINEAD. For me. You were gonna propose.

HENRY. Sure we talked about getting married.

SINEAD. I didn't know you got that far.

HENRY. Well, I did.

SINEAD. And when I went to Ciarán McGuigan's funeral, you broke up with me. And now you're giving the same ring to your new woman?

HENRY. That about sums it up, doesn't it?

SINEAD. Jane's a lucky girl – getting sloppy seconds!

HENRY. She doesn't know does she?

SINEAD. You're a cheap cunt.

HENRY. You lost my ring!

SINEAD. Well apparently I lost *my* ring.

HENRY. It's not yours. *(Under his breath.)* Doesn't even fit your fat fingers.

SINEAD. What did you say?

HENRY. I said it doesn't even fit your fat fingers!

SINEAD. Fuck you. I've had a child. What's your excuse?

HENRY. *(Proudly indicating his belly.)* What, this?

SINEAD. Yeh you fat fuck.

HENRY. Too many Feast ice creams.

SINEAD. Too much drink.

HENRY. I need one now, talking to you.

(**HENRY** *goes back to looking for the ring, he looks as* **SINEAD** *talks at him.*)

SINEAD. So you were gonna propose to me then? Had you it all planned out? Down on one knee? Come on Henry. Boat out on Lough Erne was it??

HENRY. Shut up, would ye?

SINEAD. Had you written a wee speech ? Give me all the juicy details.

HENRY. You wanna know?

SINEAD. Yeh I do!

HENRY. You really wanna know?

SINEAD. I said so didn't I?

HENRY. I was gonna do it here. Alright?

SINEAD. Here?

HENRY. Yeah. In there.

(**HENRY** *points to the Customs Hut. Beat.*)

SINEAD. Did you come here last night to propose to me?

HENRY. No!

SINEAD. We're not getting back together Henry.

HENRY. I know. But we could have done it. Got married. We could have been a proper family.

SINEAD. Me and Holly are a proper family.

HENRY. You're a half a family.

SINEAD. Don't come up here and tell me me and Holly aren't a family. / Don't do that.

HENRY. Yous aren't.

SINEAD. Are you seriously saying you and your mum weren't a family?

HENRY. Yes.

SINEAD. Jesus Henry.

HENRY. We didn't choose that, did we? You chose to end it with me.

SINEAD. Henry... I loved you.

HENRY. This is what I've been thinking about. This is why I can't propose to Jane. You were my only serious relationship. You were basically my entire family after mum died. You loved me. And you still threw it away. And I don't know why you did it. Other than you wanted out

SINEAD. That's not why I did it.

HENRY. You were just too scared to say it.

SINEAD. You know why I went to that funeral!

HENRY. Yeah I do, because there's obviously something wrong with me.

SINEAD. Jesus, it's all about you isn't it?

HENRY. You were afraid.

SINEAD. Would you just listen!

HENRY. Afraid!

SINEAD. Afraid of what?

HENRY. Afraid of being stuck with me!

SINEAD. I didn't want you to break up with me.

> (**HENRY** *snaps into* **HENRY-HOST** *as if presenting a game show.*)

HOST (H). Welcome to Family Fortunes. Sinead's gone with "She didn't want Henry to break up with her". Let's see if it's on the board.

> (*EH-EUGH! Buzzer noise from a game show..*)

Incorrect! Henry gets a chance to steal!

CONTESTANT (H). I'm going to go with "Sinead thinks I'm a total piece of shit so she pushed me away by going to that funeral".

HOST (H). Our survey says...

> (*Ding ding ding.*)

Top answer!

CONTESTANT (S). What is this shit?

HOST (H). Ooooo No swearing. There's children watching.

SINEAD. This is pointless –

HOST (H). No it's not. It's Family Fortunes!

SINEAD. You think you're always right.

HENRY. I am!

SINEAD. Let's see!

HOST (S). Welcome back to Countdown. You've joined us just in time for the Countdown Conundrum – whoever gets this right will be the winner! Here we go – BUCK-DEER-FORD. Your time starts now.

> (*Gameshow music. Jumbled up letters revealed: BUCK-DEER-FORD.*)
>
> (*Bell rings.*)

CONTESTANT (S). BORDERFUCKED!

> *("BORDERFUCKED" is presented on the screen. A round of applause.)*

CONTESTANT (H). That's not a word! Dictionary corner, dictionary corner!

SUZIE DENT. Yes! Borderfucked. Twelve letters. The condition of being fucked economically, socially, and psychologically due to the stroke of a pen. Common in Ireland, the Middle East, and all over the fucking world.

SINEAD. I won. You have to listen to me.

HENRY. No I do not.

SINEAD. Fine.

> *(Sound effects of game show music.)*

HOST (S). Welcome back to Who Wants To Be A Millionaire. We have Henry in the hot seat today, on the one million euro question.

HENRY. What is this? The Irish version? It was cancelled after two seasons.

SINEAD. Gay Byrne's an institution!

HOST (S). The question is… Will Henry shut up and let Sinead explain herself?

A: Yes

B: OK

C: Fine

D: Oisín McConville.

HENRY. I'm not answering.

HOST (S). So will it be A: Yes? Henry will shut up?

HENRY. What?

HOST (S). And let Sinead explain herself?

HENRY. You're not /even giving -

HOST (S). Final answer?

HENRY. – me a chance!

HOST (S). Final answer?!

HENRY. Fine!

(*Transition out of gameshow.*)

SINEAD. Henry, I didn't want you to dump me. I wanted to be with you. If you proposed... But I had to go to the funeral.

HENRY. Why?

SINEAD. Because I was trying to help.

HENRY. Help? It was a betrayal.

SINEAD. We have to live in this place.

HENRY. And what? Honour murderers?

SINEAD. I'm not honouring... Someone died Henry. I was there for the family.

HENRY. I don't care about his family.

SINEAD. His sister works at the youth club with me. Her brother died. I went to hold her hand.

HENRY. Boo fuckin hoo.

SINEAD. She didn't ask him to be who he was. The family needed support.

HENRY. I'd say they have plenty of support.

SINEAD. We've all been affected by this place.

HENRY. And I haven't?

SINEAD. Everyone has! Like this place is beautiful, it's class...but because of that border, people have suffered.

HENRY. What is this? Lesser Spotted Ulster?

SINEAD. It's context Henry.

HENRY. Fuck your context.

SINEAD. Ciarán McGuigan died alone. In a lake.

HENRY. He deserved it.

SINEAD. No one deserves that.

HENRY. What kind of a name is Skinny McGuigan anyway? Some Provo name.

SINEAD. His name was Ciarán!

HENRY. Do you not think some people should maybe just kill themselves?

SINEAD. What?

HENRY. Like, I know suicide is horrible and all that. But some people should just go ahead and do it.

SINEAD. Are you serious?

HENRY. They should know when they are not wanted.

SINEAD. That's disgusting.

HENRY. And if they don't cop on, then someone should tell them.

SINEAD. Tell people to kill themselves?

HENRY. Because it's not right that some bastard kills an innocent person...

SINEAD. Fuckin tell people to kill themselves?!

HENRY. ...and then gets to walk around happy go lucky.

SINEAD. He was hardly happy!

HENRY. They need to suffer.

SINEAD. He did suffer!

HENRY. D'ya know how I felt when I heard he died? I was upset.

> (Beat.)

Because I wished I'd drowned the cunt myself. I wish I'd been there to see him buck, to see him struggle, and to hold his head under the water. And look in the bastard's eyes. And say, you feel that? *(Breathes.)* That terror? You enjoy that now. Cos that's the last thing you'll ever feel.

SINEAD. It must be exhausting walking around with all that anger Henry.

HENRY. You think I enjoy it?

SINEAD. I think maybe you do.

HENRY. What?

SINEAD. Because otherwise you'd have to look at yourself. You need to get rid of that anger, Henry.

HENRY. How?

> (Beat.)

How do I do that? He killed my daddy.

> (Beat. SINEAD *doesn't have an answer.*)

SINEAD. I know Henry. I know. But I went to the funeral because it was the right thing to do.

HENRY. He was a killer.

SINEAD. He was a human being.

HENRY. That's debatable.

SINEAD. We can't carry that hatred to the grave.

HENRY. Fuck me! "Can't carry the –" So simplistic!

SINEAD. So what Henry? Just hate forever?

HENRY. Maybe we should be allowed to hate! Or do we just cover everything up? Go to killer's funerals and pretend it's all fucking gravy, eh?

SINEAD. I go to funerals on both sides.

HENRY. Both sides?! Fuck that! It's not about politics. There's such things as good and evil. Not everything has to be balanced. Bit of this, bit of that? Just cover everything up and don't look back! That's what you do.

SINEAD. What do you mean?

HENRY. You want to make this place better Sinead? Selling the land, down the youth club, greenway, tourists? You can't even come into the village – in case you see me. You've been hiding ever since you went to that funeral. Avoiding me, because you know you were wrong. You're ashamed. As you should be.

SINEAD. I'm not ashamed. I live by my ideals. I'm proud of that.

HENRY. "Ideals". Get off your high horse!

SINEAD. What?

HENRY. "Ideals". Like sending Holly to an Integrated school? "It's the way forward!" You changed your tune there.

SINEAD. That's different.

HENRY. How's it different?

SINEAD. I went cos I wanted to make things better.

HENRY. No you didn't! I know you and it's not that.

SINEAD. What is it then?

HENRY. You said all this at the time. It was almost like you couldn't understand why I didn't want you to go. How could you go and meet his family, when he'd destroyed mine? See the place packed out. Fuck, Republicans

love a funeral – more people at that funeral than at my
dad's. Like maybe I am a hateful prick – alright? I've
all this anger – fine. But I told you not to go. And you
went anyway.

SINEAD. I needed to.

HENRY. You put your ideals before me? Is that "making
things better"? Ruining our relationship?

SINEAD. No, it wasn't about –

HENRY. How can you choose ideals over a person you're
supposed to love? And I know you loved me.

>   (*Beat.*)

I know you Sinead. There has to be another reason!
Give me a real reason.

SINEAD. It was the right / thing –

HENRY. No! What is it?

SINEAD. I –

HENRY. Why did you go?

>   (*Beat.* **SINEAD** *cracks.*)

HENRY. I'm listening. Why did you go?

SINEAD. The border.

>   (*Pause.*)

HENRY. The border?

SINEAD. The border.

HENRY. The border? Border! Border border border!
Border border border border border border border.

SINEAD & HENRY. Border border. Border border border.
Border border border border border.
Border border border. Border border border border
border border border border. Border border. Border

border border. Border border border. Border border.
Border border border border border. Border border
border border border border border. Border border
border border. Border border border border border
border border. Border. Border. Border border. Border
border border border border border. Border border
border border. Border border border border border
border border. Border. Border border. Border border
border border border border border!

> (**HENRY** *snaps into* **REPORTER** *.*)

REPORTER . Sinead is down at the border where she is
going to tell me what's going on.

SINEAD. No Henry.

REPORTER . The news needs to go out Sinead!

SINEAD. I don't /want to.

REPORTER . The people need their news.

SINEAD. You can't /make me.

REPORTER . And we're live –

SINEAD. I'm not doing it!

REPORTER . – in five, four, three...

> (**HENRY** *silently gesticulates 'two' and 'one'*
> *and points at her.*)

> (**SINEAD** *stands there frozen, like a deer in the*
> *headlights.*)

FIELD REPORTER. Here I am. Down at the border where
we are getting...where we're getting reports of...reports
of...gunfire.

> (**SINEAD** *snaps into playing* **YOUNG SINEAD**
> *and* **YOUNG DAMIAN**, *as she relives the*
> *moment.* **HENRY** *watches, horrified.*)

YOUNG SINEAD. That's not fair! You're not supposed to shoot me! You're supposed to shoot the Brits!

YOUNG DAMIAN. I was shooting past you.

YOUNG SINEAD. You're a gimp Damian.

YOUNG DAMIAN. Shut up Sinead!

YOUNG SINEAD. You're a crap Provo.

YOUNG DAMIAN. I'm a great Provo!

YOUNG SINEAD. Can't shoot a Brit to save your life.

YOUNG DAMIAN. Take that back!!!

YOUNG SINEAD. *(Chants to the tune of K-I-S-S-I-N-G.)* Damian McKeever, up a tree

Waving Union Jacks 'n' sippin' English tea.

YOUNG DAMIAN. Shut up!

YOUNG SINEAD. When he met the Queen, he gave her a kiss.

How many times did he kiss the Queen?

1! 2! 3!

YOUNG DAMIAN. Shut up Sinead. I didn't kiss the Queen! Let's play something else!

YOUNG SINEAD. Stuck in the Mud! I'm on!

YOUNG DAMIAN. I'm way faster than you! You'll never get me!

YOUNG SINEAD. Yes I will!

YOUNG DAMIAN. No no no no no no!

(**YOUNG DAMIAN** *spread-eagles.*)

YOUNG SINEAD. Got you!!!

YOUNG DAMIAN. Ach! Unstick me Sinead!

YOUNG SINEAD. No!

YOUNG DAMIAN. Unstick me Sinead!

YOUNG SINEAD. You have to stay there all day.

YOUNG DAMIAN. What's that Sinead?

YOUNG SINEAD. Can't trick me!

YOUNG DAMIAN. No, look!

YOUNG SINEAD. Where?

YOUNG DAMIAN. On the fence.

YOUNG SINEAD. What is it?

YOUNG DAMIAN. It's one of the bad men. Unstick me Sinead.

YOUNG SINEAD. No. I can't look.

YOUNG DAMIAN. Help me! Sinead!

YOUNG SINEAD. I don't like it, I don't like it.

YOUNG DAMIAN. I don't wanna look at him. Help me Sinead.

UNSTICK ME! UNSTICK ME! UNSTICK ME! UNSTICK ME!

> (**HENRY** *grabs* **SINEAD** *by the shoulders to shake her out of her memory. She slowly comes back to reality. After a moment, she looks into his eyes.*)

SINEAD. That's why I went. The soldier that died here. I saw him when I was playing with Damian McKeever. He was right there.

HENRY. You found the body?

SINEAD. It wasn't that bad. But Damian...he wasn't the same after. Then years later, he killed himself. Twenty one. Same age as the soldier.

HENRY. You don't know that's why he did it.

SINEAD. It is. I know it is. Damian didn't die on the end of a belt in a wardrobe. He died right here. And I didn't even go to his funeral. Couldn't face it.

HENRY. So you went to Skinny's funeral because...what, you missed Damian's?

SINEAD. Yes, no...it's more than that.

HENRY. What then?

SINEAD. Damian killed himself. Ciarán McGuigan killed himself. Maybe that soldier did as well. And I – I want it to stop.

HENRY. Right.

SINEAD. Why do people keep giving up?

HENRY. There was nothing you coulda done.

SINEAD. I know, but it's...it's...everything. The soldier, Damian. All the young people who're dying and emigrating. I feel so guilty all the time. Guilty cos my parents had it worse than me, because I was born on the "free" side of the border, because I'm worried I'll pass this shit to Holly... Guilt cos of what I did to you. You're right, I was ashamed. I couldn't see you. I knew I'd wronged you. I dunno if I'm explaining it... But I needed to go to that funeral. I need to make sure everyone's OK all the time because otherwise I can't fuckin' handle it. Henry, it wasn't my ideals over you. It was my own messed up head over you. Am I making any sense at all?

HENRY. I think so. I mean...

SINEAD. That's why I'm selling the land. Everytime I come down here, I just... I keep thinking about the day we saw that soldier on the fence. And Damian. Stuck in the mud. I don't want to see him any more.

HENRY. Selling up won't change anything.

SINEAD. I know.

HENRY. You can't just forget about it.

SINEAD. Why not?

HENRY. Cus it happened.

(*Beat.*)

Why didn't you tell me you and Damian were there that day, that was why he...

SINEAD. I wanted to forget.

HENRY. If you told me that, I would've understood.

SINEAD. Would you?

HENRY. We could've worked it out.

(*Beat.*)

SINEAD. I don't think so.

HENRY. Why not?

SINEAD. Cos you were in so much pain, you didn't have space for mine.

HENRY. I didn't know.

SINEAD. You didn't wanna.

HENRY. I could've made space.

SINEAD. Could you? After everything? That's why we broke up Henry. Not cus I went to a funeral. Cus of who we are.

(**HENRY** *becomes more angry and unhinged over the next section. He clenches his fists and becomes more and more out of control.*)

HENRY. We never had a chance did we?

SINEAD. I dunno.

HENRY. Like, do you think we ever coulda been together?

SINEAD. Probably not.

HENRY. It's this fuckin place! I hate it, Sinead. I hate it.

SINEAD. Then leave.

HENRY. It's my home! But it's... it's too hard. I just want a normal life... Why does living where you're from have to be such a political act?

SINEAD. It just does Henry. If you're from here. It just does.

HENRY. I don't want to have to think about identity and the border and who I am. I don't want to play this fucking game anymore.

> (**HENRY** *starts to punch on the doors of the customs hut.*)

SINEAD. Stop it. Henry.

> (**HENRY** *smacks himself in the head.*)

Henry!

> (**HENRY** *tears up the stage, kicking the fence and grabbing bags of rubbish and emptying them out all over the field. As he destroys their work, the customs hut transforms into a snorting hog – the Black Pig. It snarls and seems to tower over* **HENRY** *and* **SINEAD**.*)

HENRY. It will never be better will it?

SINEAD. It will.

HENRY. I'll always be a piece of shit...

SINEAD. Henry!

HENRY. ..and this place will always be a shithole!

SINEAD. Don't do this. Look at me.

HENRY. No!

SINEAD. Look at me!

>(**HENRY** *looks.*)

Breathe.

>(**HENRY** *breathes.*)

I know you're angry. I know you're hurting. Talk to me.

HENRY. I hate myself.

SINEAD. Why?

HENRY. Cus I'm nothing.

SINEAD. No you're not.

HENRY. Yes I am. I'm nothing.

SINEAD. That's not true.

HENRY. And this place is nothing. None of us ever had a chance.

>(**HENRY** *bursts into tears.* **SINEAD** *hugs him and holds him. The pig quietens and becomes the customs hut once more. They sit together for some time.*)

SINEAD. Henry, remember the Black Pig? The Black Pig tore up the land. Cut everything open.

HENRY. Exactly.

SINEAD. Well, here's my thinking on it. The pig. It tore the souls from us. It took so much. But it gave us something too. It ripped up the land, but it's left us a path.

HENRY. A path to where?

SINEAD. I dunno Henry. Somewhere. This place isn't the edge. It's the centre. Look at what we've been through. We're not nothing.

(**HENRY** *sees something. He gets up and finds the ring. He holds it up.*)

SINEAD. You found it.

HENRY. Yeah but look at what I've done.

(*Beat.*)

Why's everything so hard?

SINEAD. We'll start again.

(**HENRY** *and* **SINEAD** *start to repair the destruction they caused.*)

(*They put the fence back up, put the rubbish back in the bin bags. They work.*)

HENRY. You know, when Dad was planning on proposing to Mum... Must have been the mid-80s. He had a friend of a friend who worked in a jewellers in Dublin. Said he could do a good deal.

SINEAD. So your dad was a cheap cunt too?

HENRY. Yup. He drove down to Dublin, on the old bumpy roads. He'd never been to Dublin in his life – terrified of the place. But he got to the jewellers. Got the ring – silver band and a sapphire.

SINEAD. Like that one.

HENRY. Like this one. So he drives back, and about a mile or two from the border he pulls over before the customs. And he's at the side of the road, looking for a place to hide the ring, so they don't see it. And you'll never guess where he puts it?

(*Beat as* **SINEAD** *looks disgusted.*)

SINEAD. He shoved it up his hole?

HENRY. Jesus, no!

SINEAD. Is that not where that was going?

HENRY. No. Eugh. Sinead!

SINEAD. You were building it up! I thought that's where /
you were going.

HENRY. It's not bloody Pulp Fiction! No! He put it in a
wee packet of Silvermints.

SINEAD. Oh.

HENRY. He even offered the customsman a mint from the
packet as he was going through.

SINEAD. No way!

HENRY. Yeah...

(Beat.)

Fuck sake, feels a bit anti-climactic now.

SINEAD. Nah nah, it was a good story. It was.

HENRY. Shoving it up his hoop would have made for a
better story.

> (**HENRY** *looks at the ring he had bought for*
> **SINEAD.** *By this time everything should have
> been cleaned up, except for the hole in the
> earth from where they were digging before.)*

Mum was buried with that ring, but when I was gonna
ask you I... I did the same thing my dad did. Drove
down to the same jewellers. And I got it for you – a
silver band with a sapphire.

> (**HENRY** *looks at the ring, before dropping it
> into the mud.* **HENRY** *lifts two spades, and
> passes one to* **SINEAD.** *The two of them bury
> the ring.)*

(Long pause.)

Well we got you sorted with that fence anyway.

SINEAD. Aye. Cheers.

HENRY. Should last. A hundred years?

SINEAD. Be lucky if it makes a hundred hours.

HENRY. As long as it lasts long enough for some big developer to buy the place, you'll be sweet.

SINEAD. Ach. Maybe I'll leave it a wee while.

(Beat.)

HENRY. Fuck, I've to tell Jane I kissed you, don't I?

SINEAD. Ho ho I'd say so. That's not going to go down well.

HENRY. You're telling me.

*(**HENRY** walks over and picks up Frederick.)*

What am I going to tell her, Frederick?

(Beat.)

SINEAD. Do you love her?

*(**HENRY** nods.)*

Go work it out then.

(Beat.)

HENRY. Everything's hard work isn't it.

SINEAD. No matter how hard you work, there's always more work to be done. Good luck.

(On either side of the fence the two of them stand at the edges of the stage.)

*(Two different phone notification sounds
repeat loudly.* SINEAD *has come into signal
range again.* SINEAD *takes out two phones
from her pocket – she's been getting messages
on both of them. She frantically tries to
understand what's going on as she scrolls
through two phones at once.)*

Fuck.

HENRY. What?

SINEAD. Shit. Henry! Can you...

HENRY. What?

SINEAD. Can you give me a hand?

HENRY. What is it?

SINEAD. Something's wrong.

HENRY. What do you mean?

SINEAD. Bubbles!

HENRY. She's calving?

SINEAD. Dad's going mad. It's coming out backwards.

HENRY. It's OK. It's OK.

SINEAD. I need to go now. Can you help us?

HENRY. Your dad can't?

SINEAD. He can barely stand. Please! It'll take two of us to
pull it out. /Come on!

HENRY. Right.

(SINEAD *grabs her things and starts to run
off.)*

But...before we go. There's one more thing I need to tell
you.

SINEAD. What?

HENRY. It was me fly tipping. That's my auld washing machine.

SINEAD. You wee prick!

> (**HENRY** *runs off.* **SINEAD** *sighs, shakes her head, and follows* **HENRY** *off, leaving the stage empty. We see the grassy hill. The old portacabin. The new fence. No rubbish. No trace.)*

> (*The sound of a magpie nearby, joined by another. The wind whispers.)*

> (*In the distance, the very faint sound of a* **COW** *calving.)*

> (*We look at the view for a long, long time.)*

> (*Until suddenly, the fence collapses.)*

> (*Blackout.)*

ABOUT THE AUTHORS'

Michael was born and raised in Belfast, where he still lives today working as an actor and a writer.

Oisín is from Warrenpoint, and works as a writer and director for stage and screen.

They met at Churchill College Cambridge, where together they ran the University Ireland Society and made theatre. For the past number of years they have worked together as a writing partnership.

Their first play *My Left Nut* was written in 2017 as part of the 'Show In a Bag' programme (Fishamble, The Irish Theatre Institute and The Dublin Fringe).

It toured Ireland and the Edinburgh Fringe, where it won a Summerhall Lustrum Award and made The Guardian's 'Best of The Fringe' list. They adapted the play into a 3-part mini-series for BBC Three. The TV series won best drama at The RTS NI Awards and was nominated for Best Drama at The Broadcast Digital Awards.

Their second play *The Alternative* was the winner of Fishamble's 'A Play for Ireland' initiative and was nominated for an Irish Times Theatre Award for Best New Play. It premiered at The Dublin Theatre Festival and toured Ireland in October 2019.

The Border Game is their third play.

For Radio, they have written *This One Time on The Border* (Radio Ulster) a six part comedy series featuring silly stories about the border, *The 100 Year Old Backstop* (BBC Radio 4) a dramatisation of the 1925 Irish Boundary Commission, and sketches for Radio Ulster's *Quick Comedy*.

Michael and Oisín are both represented by Curtis Brown.

Lightning Source UK Ltd.
Milton Keynes UK
UKHW022214270921
391271UK00007B/455

9 780573 132735